THE WRISTWATCH ALMANAC

Michael Balfour

Eric Dobby Publishing

FOR PETRA

Published by
ERIC DOBBY PUBLISHING
12 Warnford Road
Orpington
Kent BR6 6LW
ISBN: 1 85882 026 X

First published in 1994

A catalogue record of this book is available from
the British Library.

Printed and bound in Great Britain by
BPC Hazell Books Ltd
A member of
The British Printing Company Ltd

Introduction

A Rolex Oyster Perpetual Datejust chronometer with case and bracelet in 18-carat gold combined with stainless steel.

The general habit of wearing wristwatches is less than 75 years old. Yet from the very beginning of their manufacture in production line quantities, certain wristwatches have been sought after and preserved as collectors' pieces. The idea of a body adornment being useful as well as beautiful was a new one, and the early makers deliberately balanced the appeal of different watch functions with that of appearance in design. The Art Deco period coincided with a worldwide explosion in wristwatch ownership, with the happy result that there must be, tucked away forgotten at the back of drawers, many thousands of these little objects containing intricate mechanical movements which just might be worth surprisingly large amounts of money. This book is an introduction to undervalued portable antiques.

In 1992 no fewer than 877 million wristwatches were manufactured – and so it is fair to question the chances of finding collectors' pieces among that year's production. In actual fact the chances are very high for investors at the top end of the market, and reasonably good for those towards the lower end who keep a sharp look-out for limited editions from leading makers.

The Complications 18-carat yellow gold automatic skeleton wristwatch from Vacheron Constantin. A watchmaker's art fully revealed.

These makers are today almost all Swiss, and most of them have a long history. This book is probably (and somewhat surprisingly) the first inexpensive introduction to collecting wristwatches, and in it brief profiles are offered of those leading makers and some of their collectable models. As the map in this Introduction shows, the principal watchmaking centres are concentrated in north-west Switzerland, and particularly in and around the so-called Vallée de Joux. Swiss families in this region even today tend to stay in their high-sided valleys for the sake of convenient family contacts. This is why many names recur constantly in the history of Swiss watchmaking.

The design, tooling and manufacturing (which means making by hand) of watches are an extremely intense series of undertakings. For example, under Swiss law, a mechanical watch (as opposed to a quartz one) must consist of at least 120 different parts. All of them have names, and readers of this book are recommended to make constant use of the Glossary of Terms at the front, so that the 'language' of watches, which is universally used, becomes familiar.

The Swiss devotion to watchmaking has a long and remarkable history. Their most famous industry started to grow with the establishment on 19th January 1601 of the Watchmakers' Guild of Geneva. Within a century there were over 5000 watchmakers in Ge-

Contents

Acknowledgements

The great majority of the illustrations in this book were supplied by the sales and press relations departments of the makers of the watches. I sincerely thank them all for their willing co-operation and kind permission to reproduce them. I am also grateful to the following for loans of additional photographs: Christie's, Amsterdam – p.97; Christie's, London – pp.35, 80, 81, 102, 103, 134, 135; De Mesy & Company, Dallas – pp. 70, 71, 78, 79; Garrard, London – pp. 33, 42, 43, 44, 45, 52, 56, 57, 136; Watches of Switzerland, London and branches nationwide – pp. 120, 121. I took the photograph on p. 105.

Sincere thanks also to Roger Lister and Tim Bourne of Christie's, King Street, London, for all kinds of assistance, to Elisabeth Ingles for her constant encouragement and support, and to Amanda Howard for processing my manuscript with both the humour and the precision it required.

M.B.

Wristwatch Values

The capital letters within square brackets, which occur throughout this book, refer to the following bands of approximate values:

> [A] Up to £500
> [B] £500–£2,000
> [C] £2,000–£5,000
> [D] £5,000–£10,000
> [E] Over £10,000

neva, under an apprenticeship system similar to that controlled in London by The Worshipful Company of Clockmakers (founded in 1631). After the revocation of the Edict of Nantes in 1685 hundreds of Protestant Huguenots were forced into the Jura Mountains in and around La Chaux-de-Fonds. Clocks and watches were soon being assembled by hand by 'cabinotiers' from parts made in thousands of households all through the valleys. The Swiss ability to organise has to this day stood the trade in brilliant stead. Key new inventions helped to refine and perfect the movements coming out of the workshops – such as Antoine Leschaud's jewelled lever escapement (1837; developed from an English invention), Louis Audemar's stem winding and setting mechanism (1868), Georges-Frédéric Roskopf's pin-lever movement (1868), and Georges Leschot's interchangeable parts system (1868). It is said that Patek Philippe made a wristwatch in 1868 for the Hungarian Countess Kocevicz. Before this exciting 1837-1868 period France was producing the innovations – Abraham-Louis Breguet's tourbillon, and Jean-Antoine Lepine's thin movements (1770), wheels with 'wolves' teeth', watch cases with invisible hinges, and a system for setting the time at the back of a watch. These inventions came to the Swiss valleys soon enough, but were long ago preceded by the most useful one of all – that of the

The Rectangular Regulateur by Chronoswiss (1988). The three single hands are most unusual, and add to the attraction of this limited edition watch.

mainspring by Peter Henlein of Nuremberg in about 1500: it meant that clocks became portable.

Switzerland's horological history can be contrasted with the woeful fact that neither Great Britain nor the United States of America now has a single watch manufacturing company. Each has only a small number of assemblers of parts, having failed to rise to the challenges of the renewed Swiss genius for watch-making and of the Japanese talent for technical innovation and miniaturisation. Early 20th century signed wristwatches by Rotherham and J.W. Benson were English-made, but those of Sir John Bennett were Swiss.

The manufacture of pocket watches in America commenced in the 1850s, and specifically for the growing railroad system in the 1860s. Three decades later cross-country time zones were officially agreed, and the quality as well as the precision of timekeepers had to improve. At that time the prominent makers were New York Standard, Trenton, Manhattan and Knickerbocker. The most collectable makers were Lancaster Watch Company (1879-1883) and Keystone Standard (1886-1892). The leading manufacturers of pocket watches costing only one dollar or so were Waterbury Watch, Ingersoll (whose 'watch that made the dollar famous', the Yankee, came in 1895) and New Haven Clock Co. The explosive growth of the railways brought a massive upsurge in demand for watches, and mass-production methods were forced on to those manufacturers which could afford them. Not all of them could.

Only two new American companies making jewelled watches were formed after 1900: South Bend (1903), which was to merge with Columbus, and Manistee (1908). Dollar watches were dominating the market, but fresh investment in them was not forthcoming. The only new company formed specifically to make them was Bannatyne Watch Co. (1905), which was merged into E. Ingraham in 1911. Consolidation was setting in; for example, Ingersoll bought Trenton in 1907 and New England in 1912, and was then purchased itself by Waterbury Watch in 1922.

Meanwhile traditional clockmakers were entering the watch field: Westclox in 1900 and Ansonia four years later.

During about 1905 to 1929 the American pocket watch market drastically contracted, and full-scale wristwatch production commenced to compete with the suddenly flourishing Swiss trade in them. Both Elgin and Illinois introduced ladies' wristwatches in about 1906, and Gruen followed them in 1908. By 1930 the leading makers' names were Elgin, Waltham, Illinois Watch Company (which was sold to Hamilton in 1928 and whose name was used until 1953), Hampden (which ceased trading that year), Seth Thomas, Hamilton, E. Howard Watch Company (bought by Hamilton in 1931), Columbus (with South Bend which failed in 1933), and Rockford. The top dollar watchmakers were Ingersoll, Westclox, New Haven Clock Co., Waterbury Watch, Ansonia Clock, and E. Ingraham. In the middle of the market, the names were still New York Standard, Knickerbocker, Trenton, and Manhattan. Of all these famous names in American horological history, Waterbury Watch and Westclox today make clocks and lend their names to foreign watch brands, and Ingersoll and Hamilton are now Swiss-made watch brands.

Chronomètres Forget, founded in 1987 by the youthful Jean-Christophe Forget, is gaining a reputation for fine pieces such as this 18-carat gold automatic (1988). Note the unusual calendar arrangements.

Two of the Camel Trophy Adventure wristwatches, launched in 1992 and linked to the world's toughest endurance adventure. Naturally they are water-resistant, shockproof and have protected crowns.

The prominent wristwatch companies in today's marketplace may not in fact be manufacturers at all. Some oversee the assembly of commissioned parts from their own conceptions and designs, and are primarily involved in marketing exercises and the promotion of 'brands'. 'Brand' names today are positioned in the markets for wristwatches with extreme care and diligence, and they may in reality be subsidiary companies shrewdly directed towards their allotted market sectors, based on their traditions – be they sports, fashion, everyday functional, or even throwaway.

It is not widely known that the following watch 'brands' are all in the ownership of Société Suisse de Microéléctronique et d'Horlogérie SA (SMH): Blancpain, Certina, Endura, Flik Flak, Hamilton, Longines, Mido, Omega, Pierre Balmain, Rado, Swatch and Tissot. Under the vigorous, and indeed visionary, leadership of Nicolas G. Hayek, SMH has pulled together these companies, most of them with wonderful traditions, and seen to it that they each stand completely alone as 'brands', with their own promotional avenues and marketing networks. This strategy works because SMH also owns E.T.A., Habillage and Frédéric Piguet, all makers of ébauches (see **Glossary of Terms**). Vertical integration policies have become an economic necessity: for example Baume & Mercier, Cartier and Piaget are in fact under one ownership. In Japan the Hattori family control Jean Lassale, Lorus, Pulsar, Seiko and Yema Paris.

The acquisition policy of SMH has enabled some fine old names to survive. LMH (Les Manufactures Horlogères), a subsidiary of the massive German industrial conglomerate Mannesman, owns International Watch Company and a majority-holding in Jaeger-LeCoultre; in 1992 it acquired A.Lange & Söhne and intends to revive from obscurity the name of this revered old maker for new limited edition watches. The British company Accurist purchased the name and goodwill of the old Swiss maker Bueche Girod in 1989, and is reviving its traditions. For the collector these moves mean a revival of recognition of their names, and a sure increase in value of their original watches. In the case of Bueche Girod, prices of their old car radiator watches of the 1940s and 1950s will inevitably rise.

As in most leading manufacturing industries, there is an almost natural system of renewal or replacement of enterprises in Swiss watchmaking. In the spirit of the great old names, such as Audemars Piguet and Patek Philippe, new companies are coming forward with wristwatches which will unquestionably find their places in exclusive collections of the future.

These include makers such as Jean-Christoph Forget who set up his business in Geneva in 1987 at the age of 24; each of his wristwatch faces and movements is individually numbered. His first watch was a complicated 18-carat gold and stainless steel chronograph, with a day window below 12 o'clock, a date hand pointing to the outer ring and a transparent back. Its continuous bracelet or strap detaches at the top lug. Gerd R. Lang founded Chronoswiss in 1983 in Munich to make wristwatches of the highest quality from Swiss-made components. His original 1988 18-carat rose gold Rectangular Regulateur is already a collectors' piece, being limited to 650 because that is the number of old 1934 Fontainemelon calibre FHF 29 barrel-shaped movements he could find for modification.

Another name to note is that of Franck Muller, whose was born in 1958. From Genthod, near Geneva, he has been turning out complicated masterpieces. His 7200 sports chronograph is a notable achievement, and a rare commodity because it is limited to just 50 pieces. Daniel Roth has French origins and trained for 10 years with Breguet; since 1988 he has been making extremely expensive complicated watches in just one unusual shape in Le Sentier in the Vallée de Joux, and his tourbillons are already sought after in exclusive outlets. It is noteworthy that, in the spirit of Breguet, guilloché dials are a constant feature of wristwatches by Forget, Chronoswiss, Muller and Roth.

In so many ways past traditions fuel present transitions – but how far back do wristwatches in fact go? In the accounts books of Jaquet-Droz & Leschot, makers in Geneva, there is mention of a 'watch to be fixed to a bracelet' under the year 1790. It is widely recorded that the Empress Josephine once wore a jewelled bracelet on each wrist in 1806, and both incorporated a watch – one showing the time of the day and the other the calendar date. Mass production of wristwatches began in the early 1880s, and it was provoked by orders from the German Navy for its officers. It is a surprising fact that about 93,000 wristwatches were sold in Germany in 1902; the figure for 1907 was some 400,000. That was the year when the American makers Elgin and Illinois began manufacturing them on a large scale.

Wars so often produce irreversible changes in habits. Before 1914 civilian men rejected the notion of wearing such a fancy object as a timekeeper on a bracelet or strap on their wrists. In Britain, Oscar Wilde's very public example of such dress behaviour was widely noticed. However, turn-of-the-century haute couture fashion - first in Paris and then in London and elsewhere in Europe's capitals – dictated that jewelled timepieces on the wrist were new and acclaimed accessories. They were beautiful and they were useful.

Trench warfare during the First World War changed

men's attitudes to wristwatches forever. First the officers and later ordinary ranks found them essential for synchronised action – and so they have been ever since. In fashion centres throughout Europe in the increasingly frivolous Roaring '20s watch designs for gentlemen's models 'loosened up' and steadily became fashion objects. After all they did enshrine unbelievably small motors that required winding up only once a day, would often withstand shocks and were sometimes, after the mid-1920s, even resistant to immersion in water.

Popularity in the 1920s brought volume production to Switzerland permanently, and as the lines extended so also a contraction in whole-of-the-watch manufacture commenced. The days of front-room parts-making in small villages in and around the Jura Mountains were passing. Large specialist component suppliers were establishing their factories, and the best makers – as portrayed in this book – were by the 1970s reaching out for partners, to survive the 'quartz' revolution. The powerful SMH group grew out of this suddenly difficult situation, and then of course the famously successful Swatch helped steer the company into enduring prosperity.

There is no doubt at all that there will always be a market among collectors for both new and used me-

Omega Speedmasters were worn by American astronauts on 21st July 1969, as exemplified in this display photograph, in the first moon landing. They had Velcro straps.

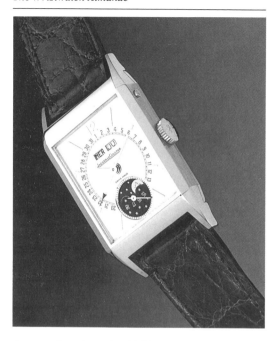

An unusual mechanical gold-filled Jaeger-LeCoultre wrist-watch has a silvered dial with dot numerals and a moonphase indicator within. The red-pointed hand, adjusted by the second lower crown, gives the date in the month.

chanical watches of distinction. Leading makers of them are all featured in this book. In this age of technical wizardry clear new trends in wristwear can be seen; Citizen's catalogue contains miniature marvels. But they are not merely timepieces, and young collectors will shortly be looking out for truly innovatory watches with complications of a quite different nature to those of Audemars Piguet, Patek Philippe, etc. In 1993 Casio produced its CMD-10. From this wristwatch all the normal functions of a television or video can be controlled. And it also tells the time.

MICHAEL BALFOUR
London

Glossary of Terms
(American terms in italics)

ANALOGUE (*ANALOG*)
Time indication by dial and hands. Was once an electronic term; now used in watchmaking with advent of quartz watch.

ANTIMAGNETIC
Protected from all but strongest magnetism; quartz watches cannot be affected by magnetism.

APERTURE - *see* Window

APPLIED NUMERALS OR MARKERS
Raised metal characters attached to dial, by adhesion or screws.

ARABIC NUMERALS
0, 1, 2, 3, 4, 5, 6, 7, 8, 9. Originated in India; introduced to Europe about 1000 years ago.

ARBOR
Axle (staff) upon which wheels of train are mounted.

ART DECO
Design style influenced by cubist geometry, broadly between 1910 and 1935. Baguette-shaped case often used.

AUTOMATIC WATCH
Mechanical watch with mainspring that is wound by wearer's movements, via a rotor.

AUXILIARY DIAL (*REGISTER*)
Small dial showing seconds only, up to one minute, generally at six o'clock position.

BACK or BOTTOM PLATE
Furthest from dial.

BACK WINDER
Flat crown set into back of case for winding and changing time.

BAGUETTE
Rectangular case shape with length at least three times width.

BALANCE
Running regulator of mechanical watch; it oscillates about its axis of rotation; balance spring (hair-spring) makes it swing to and fro ('tick-tock') in equal time parts. Balances (often bi-metallic) of modern wristwatches have up to ten beats per second.

BAND
Centre ring of case into which movement fits; front and back bezels are hinged to it.

BARREL
Circular box containing mainspring; teeth attached at edge drive gears; going barrel has great wheel mounted on it.

BATON NUMERALS
Undecorated non-numerical markers of hours, minutes and seconds.

BEAT
Sound of ticking of watch caused by teeth of escape wheel striking pallets or arms of escapement.

BEVELLED (*BEVELED*)
Deviation from flat surface, forming straight slant.

BEZEL
Metal surround frame in which crystal (glass) is fitted.

BI-METALLIC
Two different metals (eg: steel and brass) fused or riveted together to make single strip for balances; prevents variations in temperature affecting movement.

BREGUET HAND
Popular design by Breguet; slightly tapered needle of hand ends in pointed head beyond hollow circle. Sometimes called moon hand.

BRIDGE
Upper metal plates that hold pivots or jewels in place in movement. Always with two or more feet or supports.

BUBBLEBACK
Popular name for early Rolex Oyster Perpetual (about 1930 on).

BUTTON
Better known as a crown (winder).

CABOCHON
Decorative stone set in crown.

CALIBRE (*CALIBER*)
Once used only to denote the size of movement; now often only indicates version (eg: gentlemen's, ladies', automatic). Generally given with manufacturer's name. From Latin qua libra (weight), or from Arabic kalib (mould).

CARAT (*KARAT*)
Pure gold is 24 carat. 18 carat is alloy of 18 parts pure gold.

CASE
Housing for movement, dial and crystal.

CENTRE (*CENTER*) or SWEEP SECONDS
Seconds hand rotating at centre of dial, concentric with hour and minute hands, indicating seconds at edge of dial.

CHAPTER RING
Circle of hour indicators.

CHRONOGRAPH
Watch which has independent stop mechanism for short interval timing. Common types are one-button, using crown, or separate button above it; two-button, top button stopping and starting time-measuring function and bottom one for resetting it; 12 hour with moon phase; split second.

CHRONOMETER
Watch which has gained Official Timing Certificate after precision and reliability tests in official observatory, as ruled by Swiss Federation of Watch Manufacturers.

COMPLICATED WATCH
Watch with additional functions not related to time of day (eg: calendar, chronograph, moonphase, perpetual, repeater).

CROWN (*WINDER*)
Knob, generally round, knurled and positioned outside case at 3 o'clock, for winding and setting.

CRYSTAL
Glass dial cover, made of glass, plastic, synthetic sapphire or quartz crystal, fitted into bezel.

CUSHION SHAPE
Square with rounded edges.

DATE APERTURE
Window in dial showing date.

DAUPHINE HAND
Diamond-shaped, with point greatly stretched towards numerals.

DEAD-BEAT ESCAPEMENT
Escapement ensuring hands do not recoil after jumping.

DEPLOYMENT BUCKLE
Two strips of hinged metal (curved to wrist shape) on watchband; one folds over the other, on closing, to cover it.

DETENT
Any locking device in movement.

DETENT ESCAPEMENT
Escapement employing detent to hold up escape wheel.

DEVIATION
Time discrepancy.

DIAL or FACE
Front of watch, showing hours, minutes and seconds. Other small dials are auxiliary or subsidiary.

DIAMETER
Dimension used for measuring watch size.

DIGITAL WATCH
Indication of time displayed by numerals only.

DIVER'S WATCH
Water-resistant.

DOCTOR'S WATCH
Also known as duo-dial or duo-plan. Auxiliary seconds dial is separate from hour and minute dial; useful for quick reference.

DOME
Second cover inside back of watch.

DUAL-DIAL - *see* **Doctor's Watch**

EBAUCHE
French word commonly used. Incomplete movement ready for addition of escapement, timing system and mainspring.
ELECTRIC WATCH
Watch using electric contacts, coils, condensers or registers, in which closed circuits balance impulse.
ELECTRONIC WATCH
Quartz watch, with semi-conductive elements like transistors.
ENGINE-TURNED
Machine engraving, like etching.
ESCAPE WHEEL
Last wheel in going train, working with pallet fork to control rate.
ESCAPEMENT
Parts of movement which convert rotary motion of gear train into precise 'to-and-fro' motion.
FACE - see Dial
FEUILLE HAND
Extended leaf-like shape.
FORM WATCH
Watch in shape of something unrelated to its function.
FORMED MOVEMENT
Watch movement that is not round.
FOURTH WHEEL
Generally wheel carrying seconds hand and driving escape wheel. Fourth wheel from great wheel in going train.
FRAME
Plates and pillars in movement.
FREQUENCY
Numbers, generally expressed as Hertz (Hz), of cycles, oscillations, periods or vibrations per second.
GEARS
Toothed wheels (20 to 100 teeth, in brass) and pinions (six to 12 teeth, in steel), operating together.
GLASS - *see* Sapphire
GOING BARREL
Contains spring which is wound in same direction as drive.
GOLD
Yellow, pink or white, used for cases and bracelets. 24-carat pure gold is yellow; alloys change colour.
GOLD-PLATED - *see* Rolled Gold
GRANDE SONNERIE
Strikes previous hour before each quarter.
GREAT WHEEL
First (and largest) in gear train.
GUILLOCHÉ
Engine-turned. Machine engraving, like etching.

HACK FEATURES *or* **BALANCE STOPPING**
Seconds hand which is stopped in order to synchronise time when crown is pulled out.

HAIRSPRING *or* **BALANCE SPRING**
Spiralled spring attached to balance to control speed of oscillations.

HALF-HUNTER
Glass half covered by hinged case extension.

HERTZ
Convention for expressing numbers of cycles, oscillations, periods or vibrations per second. Often abbreviated to Hz, KHz (1,000 Hz) or MHz (1,000,000 Hz). Named after German physicist Heinrich Rudolf Hertz (1857-94).

HOROLOGY
Science of timekeeping.

HUNTER
Glass completely covered by hinged case extension (often spring-loaded). Also known as savonette watch.

INCABLOC
Shock absorber

INTEGRAL BRACELET
Natural extension of watch-case design.

JEWELS
Used as bearings to reduce wear and abrasion at points of greatest friction in movements. Commonly 15 to 18 are used (quantity does not indicate quality or value of watch). Once, natural rubies and sapphires were used; most jewels are now synthetic.

JUMP HOUR
Hour hand which moves forward once each hour; or hour appears once each hour in a window.

LCD
Liquid crystal display, of numerals in bars, continuously, in electronic digital watch.

LED
Light-emitting diode, to display (not continuously) numerals in electronic digital watch.

LÉPINE CALIBRE (*CALIBER*)
Calibre in which movement has only one plate, to which each wheel is supported by a separate cock. Invented by Jean Antoine Lépine (1720-1814); perfected by Breguet for ultra-thin watches.

LEVER *or* **ANCHOR ESCAPEMENT**
Brass or steel escapement part of mechanical watch, impulsing at each vibration, shaped like anchor. Invented by Thomas Mudge (1715-94) in 1754.

LIGNE *(expressed as ''')*
One inch is one ligne, or one-twelfth of a French foot (ie: 2.256mm). Lignes (or lines) are used for indicating wristwatch movement sizes, commonest being between 5.5 and 13. American sizes are based on 30ths of an inch. Dimension is diameter of lower plate (beneath dial); in formed movements diameter is smallest axis.

LOSANGE HAND
Small diamond shape before sharp point; beyond stem with bulge.

LUG (HORN)
Part or parts of watch case to which band, bracelet or strap is attached.

LUMINOUS
Giving off light. Radium used c.1900-1930s (now illegal).

MAINSPRING
Principal spring in watch; flat and coiled in barrel. Drives train wheels.

MEAN TIME
Average length of all solar days in year; usual time shown by watches.

MECHANICAL WATCH
Driven by spring with vibratory system which runs mechanically (such as balance or pendulum).

MINUTE REPEATER
Repeating watch that sounds hours, quarters and additional minutes.

MONTH APERTURE
Window in dial displaying month, generally abbreviated.

MOON PHASE WATCH
Watch displaying phase of moon (often in blue) through 29.5 days; correction for extra 44 minutes per month often incorporated.

MOTION WORK
Gear train for moving hour hand.

MOVEMENT
Complete mechanism of watch; from 120 to over 600 parts may be incorporated.

OSCILLATION
'To-and-fro' swing between two extreme positions (- see also Balance).

OYSTER CASE
Rolex watch with water-resistant case.

PAVÉ
'Paved with', as in dial covered with stones.

PALLET
Small jewel for locking escape wheels; receives impulses to impart to oscillator.

PALLET FORK
Jewel-tipped lever in escapement; in conjunction with balance and escape wheel.

PERPETUAL (sometimes ETERNAL)
Self-winding automatic movement.

PERPETUAL CALENDAR
Calendar mechanism with display which corrects itself for long and short months and leap years. Formula adjustments for variations in Gregorian calendar continue only until 28 February 2100. That is not a leap year, so manual changes will have to be made to all but most complicated watches. 2200, 2300, 2500, 2600 and 2700 will not be leap years either.

PILLAR
Post separating plates in movement.

PINION
Small toothed wheel.

PIVOT
Ends of arbor (staff) mounted in jewels or plates, enabling arbor to revolve.

PLATES
Parallel flat plates between which wheels of gear train are pivoted.

PLATINUM
Precious silver-white metal; heavier than gold.

POWER RESERVE INDICATOR (*UP AND DOWN INDICATOR*)
Hand or window showing remaining hours of power.

QUARTER REPEATER
Repeating mechanism which sounds hours and quarters.

QUARTZ
Rock crystal (silicon dioxide) made to oscillate by electronic switching. Maintains constant frequency according to its cut. Synthetic quartz crystals are now used.

RAISED NUMERALS OR MARKERS - see APPLIED
RESERVE
Running time left after watch is fully wound.

ROLLED GOLD (*GOLD-FILLED*)
Very thin sheet of hot gold bonded on to backing metal.

ROMAN NUMERALS
Besides arabic, most common numerals used. I, II, III, IIII (not IV), V, etc.

ROSE (sometimes PINK or RED) GOLD
24-carat (pure yellow) gold alloyed with copper.

ROSKOPF WATCH
Simplified mechanical watch invented in 1867 at La Chaux-de-Fonds by G.F.Roskopf (1813-89). Has unusual gear train, and generally without jewels.

ROTOR
In automatic watches, rotor winds mainspring; in quartz watches, it is permanently rotating magnet in step-switch motor.

RUBY
Term for corundum, a synthetic stone. It is used to reduce wear on some pivots.

SAPPHIRE
Scratchproof glass over dial now made of synthetic sapphire.

SAVONETTE
European term for hunter watch.

SELF-WINDING
Watch with spring winding mechanism tightened by wrist movement. Four hours' activity produces about 30 hours' running time.

SHOCK-RESISTANT WATCH
Judged to be shock-resistant if, when dropped on to hard surface from height of 3 ft (1m) it does not stop, or if its daily rate does not afterwards change by more than 60 seconds.

SIDEREAL TIME
Standard of time used by astronomers, determined by rotation of earth relative to stars; sidereal day is three minutes and 55.5 seconds shorter than mean solar day.

SIGNED MOVEMENT
Signature on movement of its maker, which might not be same as that on dial.

SKELETON WATCH
Dial of skeleton watch has separate chapter ring with interior removed, leaving only numerals and exposing wheels and interior reduced mechanisms of movement. Back plate also cut away and fitted with glass.

SOLAR TIME
As shown by sundial and uncorrected.

SPLIT SECOND CHRONOGRAPH
Chronograph with sweep seconds hand, independent of time hands.

STEM
Shaft connecting winding mechanism to crown.

STERLING SILVER
Minimum purity of English silver is 925 parts in 1000.

STOP WATCH - see Chronograph

STOP WORK
Device on barrel controlling number of winding turns, thus preventing overwinding.

SUBSIDIARY DIALS
Smaller auxiliary dials, indicating elapsed minutes and running seconds.

SUNK SECONDS
Subsidiary dial depressed into main dial to avoid interference with hour and minute hands.

SWEEP SECONDS - see Centre Seconds

'SWISS MADE'
1971 Swiss Federal government ordinance decrees that 'Swiss Made' expression can only be on watch and used in marketing if (i) at least 50 per cent of components by value, excluding costs of assembly, are of Swiss manufacture, (ii) it was assembled in Switzerland, (iii) it was started up and regulated by its manufacturer in Switzerland, and (iv) it is subject to continuing legal obligation of technical inspection in Switzerland.

TACHYMETRE (*TACHOMETER*)
Speed or revolution measuring system as outer ring or on bezel.

TANK CASE
Now common name for severe rectangular case shape; originally exclusive name of Cartier wristwatch, and patented by Gruen.

TIMEPIECE
Any watch which does not strike or chime.

TONNEAU
Case shape with wide centre and flat tapered ends.

TOURBILLON
Invention by Breguet for preventing vertical position errors, with revolving platform which goes through all positions, thus neutralising them.

TRAIN
Wheels and pinions of watch, transmitting power from great (first) wheel to escapement. Variations in numbers of teeth affect running time and oscillations.

TRITIUM
Luminous paint for dials, numerals or markers and hands.

TUNING FORK
Transistor switching between two magnets, oscillating 360 times a second, to regulate smooth running. High frequency gives greater precision.

ULTRA-THIN (*EXTRA-FLAT*)
Unusually thin movement, and always less than 3mm thick.

VERGE ESCAPEMENT
Early, simple and common escapement.

VERMEIL
Gilded silver.

WATERPROOF (*WATER-RESISTANT*)
Illegal term in USA. Waterproof watches, sold as such, must withstand water pressure at depth of 1m (3.28ft) for 30 minutes and thereafter for 90 seconds at 20m (65.6ft).

WHEEL TRAIN
First (great) wheel, which supplies power; second (centre) wheel, turns once an hour and carries minute hand; third wheel transmits power to fourth wheel, which can carry seconds hand; escape wheel.

WHITE GOLD
24-carat (pure yellow) gold alloyed with nickel.

WINDOW
Aperture on dial, to show day, date, month or digit.

WORLD TIMER
Watch showing current time in any city or time zone, according to model.

This Salvador Dali 'crash' watch (1991) was designed by Philippe Muller after he saw Dali's famous surreal painting 'The Disintegration of the Persistence of Memory'. This Softwatch is by Exeaquo of Geneva.

COLLECTING HINTS

An unusual jump hour watch from Breguet, the company bearing the name of probably the greatest ever watchmaker - Swiss-born Abraham-Louis Breguet (1747-1823). This automatic has a platinum case.

The soundest approach to starting to collect wristwatches is via the salerooms of auctioneers. Catalogues are there to tell you much of what you need to know, and the lots of watches are on display for anyone to examine. Also experts are at hand to answer questions and advise. Actually handling a wristwatch will always tell you more than any illustration can. So, to start off, attend as many sales previews as you can and then the subsequent auctions, so that you begin to get a feel for the market you are about to enter.

At some sales you will come across runs of watch and clock journals. The oldest English one is the monthly trade magazine Horological Journal, founded in 1858 by The British Horological Institute (see **Useful Addresses** on page 140) and long before wristwatches entered its pages. Antiquarian Horologist (1953) is concerned only with clocks. The best magazine for wristwatch collectors is the colourful International Wristwatch (1989), which is published in London and also elsewhere as international editions of the Italian Orologi da Polso. This bi-monthly publication profiles a number of prominent makers in each issue, and so will eventually guide you towards

Limited edition collectors should note this Hublot automatic mechanical 18-carat gold chronograph. Launched in 1993, the edition is limited to 250 pieces.

preferred makers. It also offers private collectors free classified advertising as well as previews and reviews of auction sales. For up-to-date watch trade news buy Retail Jeweller (1963), the official journal of the National Association of Goldsmiths. There is no wristwatch collectors' club in Great Britain; some exist on the Continent, and one flourishes in America (again, see **Useful Addresses** on page 140).

Money and unnecessary effort can be saved if you decide on the profile of your new watch collection before you commence to buy. It is unlikely that you will choose to buy new watches of any sort (unless collecting new Swatches as they appear appeals to you). Remember that in 1992 about 1,000 million new watches were manufactured around the world (Citizen, of Japan, alone made 186.7 million in the year to March 1993). The advent of quartz-powered watches at the beginning of the 1970s threw the very old-established and highly traditional hand-made and assembled Swiss watch industry into disarray as their sales plunged. The Swiss rose to this challenge magnificently. Not only did they produce the all-conquering quartz Swatch, but they updated their methods of making mechanical watches, expanded ranges of the fine old names, reduced prices, sold more aggressively, and won back market share. The result, for the wristwatch collector, is that mechanical watches are more popular than ever, more accessible in the market place, and yet not produced in high enough numbers of each model to dilute their appeal. A mechanical wristwatch must, by Swiss legal definition, contain a minimum of 120 different parts; over 1,850 separate operations are involved in its manufacture, with the use of over 1,000 tools. These facts partly explain why only a few thousand at most of famous models are ever produced – which makes them so collectable. Also many of them bear serial numbers, of which their makers maintain records; so, as with chassis numbers of classic cars, such watches start with a known pedigree, and this too is attractive to collectors.

The most elaborate mechanical watches, which are expensive, are called 'complicated' and they fall into six categories: the (quite simple) chronometer, the moonphase calendar, the perpetual calendar, the ultra-thin chronograph, the minute repeater, and the tourbillon regulator (see **Glossary of Terms** on pages 15-24). Complicated watches are always going to be costly, but a further factor for collectors to note is that case metals vary. Top of the range models may be in 14, 18 or 22-carat yellow, pink or white gold, or perhaps in platinum, silver gilt (called vermeil) or titanium. Stainless steel cases have less appeal, but some collectable models are only found in stainless steel.

Many prospective collectors of wristwatches eventually settle, after many hours in auction rooms, among dealers and in armchairs reading up their horology, upon a particular theme. There are many to choose from, and here are some 'signatures' (names on dials, which may not be the actual manufacturers' own) to look out for.

Alarm watches. Solutions to the problem of producing a loud constant sound from a small mechanism. Eterna's first models (1912-14, making them among the earliest mass-produced watches); Vulcain's Cricket (1947); LeCoultre's Memovox (1951);

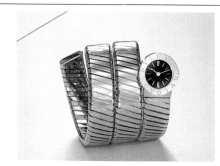

Bulgari has been producing watches since the 1940s. This is the three-colour gold Snake Watch, incorporating a bezel design which dates back to Bulgari's first volume production in the late 1970s.

Pierce's Duofon (1956); Paul Buhré's Alarm (1956-57); Vulcain's Golden Voice, for ladies (1958).

Automatic watches. Early classics which are hard to find. Harwood (an English 'first' in 1926); Rolls (1930); Glycine (1931); Wig-Wag (1931); Harwood's Autorist (1931); Rolex Perpetual (1931). Other names from the 1938-48 period: Burron, Certina; Cyma; Felsa; Eterna; Omega; Pierce; A.Schild; Tissot; Zenith.

Car watches. Some very attractive 1930s models can be found, but not often in good condition because they tended to be worn daily by their original sporting owners. Aston Martin; Bugatti (Bueche Girod); Buick (Mido); Ferrari (Cartier), RS27 (Motochron; limited to 1580; recent); Rolls-Royce (Blancpain, in both gentlemen's and ladies' sizes); Lancia (Bueche Girod); Lagonda; Mercedes (Bueche Girod; Jean Eté).

Cartoon character watches. These were (and are) inexpensive; the early ones had printed cardboard dials. Alice in Wonderland; Annie (Get Your Gun) Oakley; Bambi; Batman; Boy Scout; Cinderella; Davy Crockett; Donald Duck; Goofy; Hopalong Cassidy; L'il Abner; Lone Ranger; Mickey Mouse (this was the first of them, produced by Ingersoll in America in 1933); Minnie Mouse; Pinocchio; Popeye; Roy Rogers and Trigger; Superman; Winnie the Pooh; Wonder Woman; Woody Woodpecker; Zorro. Most new 'blockbuster' films in recent years have spawned a 'tie-in' wristwatch.

Designer watches. All these fashion-accessory watches are commissioned from large Swiss manufacturers and generally come in both gentlemen's and ladies' sizes. Benetton; Burberry; Carven; Chanel; Christian Dior; Christian Lacroix; Dunhill; Fiorucci; Gianni Versace; Giorgio; Gucci; Guy Laroche; Léonard; Hermès; Karl Lagerfeld; Lanvin; Pierre Balmain; Pierre Cardin; Rochas; Tiffany; Yves St Laurent.

Swatches. This is the fun category. Many hundreds of models have appeared since March 1983; this pioneering wholly Swiss counter-challenge to the Japanese quartz watch invasion in the 1970s has proved to be a brilliant and enduring marketing success. The earliest and the limited edition models are the most collectable, and they have to be in complete original packaging and in mint condition. The Kiki Picasso was launched in 1985 at US$40; it is now valued at about US$40,000. Collection albums are available.

Jewellers' own signature watches. Asprey; Boucheron; Bulgari; Cartier (in a special category of its own); Chaumet; Collingwood; Garrard; Graff; Mappin & Webb; Tessiers; Tiffany; Van Cleef & Arpels.

L.E.D watches. In the early 1970s light emitting diode watches were considered trendy – very flash, with vulgar coloured steel cases, red glass and requiring both your hands to reveal the digital time. Bulova; Pulsar.

Limited editions. This is a popular category in all fields of collecting; each individually numbered. Andy Warhol's Times/5 (Movado 1988; 250 made); Georges Piaget (Piaget 1992; 500 made: 200 in yellow gold, 150 in white gold, 100 in platinum, 50 in pink gold; each signed as well as numbered); Chronographe Antimagnétique (Rolex 1956; 100 made); 'Vegetables' Swatch series of three (Swatch 1991; 333 made of each); El Primero 1291/1991 moon phase watch (Zenith 1991; 250 made, to celebrate Switzerland's 700th anniversary). Almost every maker has produced wristwatches in limited editions.

Masonic watches. In unique and attractive shapes and often highly decorative.

Military watches. These evolved very quickly for use by officers in the First World War for synchronisation in trench warfare, and were directly responsible for bringing wristwatches into universal everyday use. Before then they were considered somewhat effeminate. The world's earliest known mass-production watch was that of Girard-Perregaux for German naval officers in 1880, with a four-by-four protective metal grille over the glass dial. Eterna; Girard-Perregaux; Ingersoll; Movado; Omega; Waltham.

Novelty watches. For less than very serious collectors of wristwatches this is another area which offers amusement. Originality, as well as a degree of rarity of course, are the only points of cohesion about such a collection, and they might not increase the value of it as a whole when put up for sale. On the other hand a ready-made assembly of nice examples of rare oddities might be very appealing to a new and wealthy collector. Reverso (Jaeger-LeCoultre 1931; created for English polo players, and still being made); Speech Synthesizers (Seiko 1983); Rock watches (Tissot 1985); Automatic self-winders (Harwood 1926); Ingenieur (IWC 1946); Accutron (Bulova, with tuning fork 1965); Watches with minute hands only (Revue Thommen); Wood watches (Lacher); Watches with hinged back (Swiss Tonic; for pills and condoms); Museum Watch (Movado; early mechanical version 1961); Chronoswiss (Cabrio); Rolex (early) bubble backs; Movado Polyplans (from 1912); Desk clock/wristwatch (Borel Fils & Co, c.1935); Hitler Watch (with his picture and the words 'Deutschland erwache', c.1933).

The stepped single lugs indicate that this is in fact a Reverso. It was made under licence in the late-1930s for E. Gübelin by Jaeger-LeCoultre. Compare it with the front cover.

Sporting watches. Select a pursuit with which you are already familiar. Yachting: Admiral's Cup (Corum), Tidal Chronometer (Krieger, USA); Polo (Baume & Mercier, Jaeger LeCoultre, Piaget); Flying: Lindbergh (Longines), Wingman (Citizen), Flightmaster (Omega), Aerospace (Breitling); Diving: Aqualand (Citizen), Captain Nemo (Hermès), 6000 Series (TAG-Heuer); Mountaineering: Altichron (Citizen), Bivouac (Favre-Leuba); Golf: L'Open (Gérard Genta); Car Racing: Mille Miglia (Corum); Car Rallying (Breitling); Motoring (Biforca, c. 1970); Windsurfing: Series 1000/2000/3000 (TAG-Heuer); Hunting: Gefica Safari (Gérald Genta). Oris have produced the Player's watch which keeps four separate scores at once, independent of the time of the day.

Care and maintenance: Everything connected with the purchase of a wristwatch should be retained and stored out of direct daylight: receipt, packaging, certificate, guarantee, etc. These assist both with a resale and insurance.

Christie's print the following note at the front of their catalogues: 'Please note that most wristwatches with water-resistant cases have been opened to identify type and quality of movement. It cannot be assumed that the watches are still waterproof, and purchasers are advised to have the watches checked by a compe-

Omega's automatic Seamaster Professional Chronograph, with both the case and bracelet in titanium.

tent watchmaker before use.' It is important never to open the back of an expensive watch yourself. Apart from the effect on water-resistance, dust will enter and the movement will be disturbed. A qualified watch repairer should maintain an expensive watch, which should otherwise reside on its owner's wrist where it will be an object of both beauty and use. Just remember to check the condition of the strap or bracelet occasionally.

...and finally

For some reason gentlemen's watches are more sought after and collectable than the same models in ladies' sizes.

BUYING AND SELLING

To celebrate their 150th year as Crown jewellers in 1993, Garrard commissioned a limited edition of 150 of this Anniversaire watch from Patek Philippe. It is an ultra-thin automatic in 18-carat rose gold and has a transparent back plate. It was priced at £7,950, sold out immediately and is already a more valuable collectors' piece.

After you have decided upon a category of wristwatches to collect, and had a good look around markets and auction houses to establish their broad price bands (see page 4) and availability, it is time to commence the formation of your collection.

Shops, street markets and boot sales

Most high streets have a jeweller's and many of them are long-established family businesses with reputations for their horological knowledge and expertise, dependability and integrity. They stock new wristwatches for, on the whole, the lower end of the market along with clocks, jewellery, silverware and other gift items. For an extensive range of more expensive new pieces Watches of Switzerland have many branches in London and also around the country. Like many smaller shops they offer engraving and valuation services. Watches of Switzerland also offer a two-year guarantee, and the first-year maintenance service is free. Other up-market London stockists include Aspreys, Garrard and Mappin & Webb.

This rose gold automatic from Audemars Piguet is the Star Wheel. The power reserve indicator is the left subsidiary dial.

Wristwatch dealers can first be identified through classified trade directories and journals, and then confirmed as prominent and hopefully reputable through their regular advertisements. You may even come to recognise some dealers in the sale rooms because there are not many of them. A good wristwatch dealer will understand your request for a full descriptive dated receipt for a purchase, and for your desire for the original box in which it was supplied, together with any relevant certificate and guarantee. The serial number of a prominent watch make can be useful later on for confirmation of provenance. If the wristwatch you are thinking of buying is a 'complicated' one, ask the dealer to demonstrate to you all its functions and then go through them yourself with him.

You might, on the other hand, have decided to invest modestly at the lower end of the market. This means combing street stalls on market days and car boot sales. There the ground rules are different and simpler. Sellers' ignorance can lead to real bargains (but you might not get a receipt); watches subsequently discovered to be fakes (from Hong Kong and Taiwan; 'funny' Rolexes are especially common) can lead to bad tempers. Watches found to be stolen can mean bad consciences or real legal problems. Buying and selling privately in public markets should be accompanied by mutual agreements that 'what you see is what you get'. In these conditions the scent of a bargain can sometimes be easy to pick up; for example an inscription on the back of a watch might feature a well-known public personality which the seller has failed to recognise. 'Association' watches are certainly desirable.

Auctions

The serious collector is on safer ground in the sale rooms of large auctioneers. Christie's and Sotheby's are the most prominent in Britain; Phillips have also sale rooms around the country, and Bonhams hold frequent watch and clock auctions in London (see **Useful Addresses** on page 140). All respectable auctioneers hold preview days – two or more and sometimes on a Sunday as well. It is important to spend time at these, and not to hesitate to ask for expert advice and help when you need it. If you do not subscribe annually for wristwatch catalogues or feel the need to buy one on a preview day, there is always one there to consult freely. It really is advisable to acquire the catalogue of a sale in which you are interested beforehand. Not only can you then study the small print of its Conditions of Sale, but you can make your own notes as you look at the lots and become familiar with the trade 'language' used in the

The distinctive Olympos from Zodiac. Other collectable Zodiac wristwatches include the Dynotron (1968) and the Astrographic (1969) with its new power reserve indicator.

Some of the inexpensive Harrods Watches which were launched in a series of twelve in December 1993. Their colourful modern designs were inspired by distinctive features in various departments of the London store.

watch descriptions (see **Glossary of Terms** on pages 15-24). Most of the other preview browsers will most likely be dealers (as opposed to collectors simply), so look out for their particularly close and careful inspections (and catalogue scribbles!).

One of the many advantages of subscribing annually to wristwatch auction catalogues is that you will also receive lists of the prices obtained. Remember also that these generally include buyers' premiums charged by the sale rooms; these range from 10% to 15% of the 'hammer price' (and upon which VAT at the standard rate is payable). If the buyers' premium is 15% divide the inclusive price listed by 1.15 to obtain the 'hammer price'. You can compare these with pre-sale estimates as printed in catalogues; soon you will detect trends, and spots the surprises and disappointments. Unsold lots will not be noted. Traditionally, auctioneers pitch their estimates on the low side, but remember that these do not of course include buyers' premiums.

Buying and selling at auction is necessarily more complicated than a friendly trade at a car boot sale, but for a serious investor in a wristwatch collection the rules and commissions are generally worth their trouble and expense. Buying in a Christie's auction, for example, involves paying a 15% buyers' premium (plus VAT) on a lot hammer price up to £30,000; it drops to 10% on any higher lot price. On some lots (denoted as such in the catalogue) VAT is payable on hammer prices as well; the tax is refundable if the goods are subsequently exported outside the European Union. If you have bid successfully for a lot you can pay for it immediately and carry off your new prize. In any case you are generally required to pay within two days - unless you are a substantial customer at the largest auction houses, when you might have up to 30 days' credit (an invaluable re-sale period for dealers).

Bidding at auctions among the professionals can be a nervous undertaking. Christie's alleviate this with the use of 'paddles'. When you arrive in the sale room you register your name, address and bank details and then receive a large hand-held paddle bearing your personal bidder's number. You simply hold it aloft to record your bid; if it is the final and successful one then your paddle number is called out by the auctioneer - and your wristwatch lot has commenced its

Georg Jensen commenced watchmaking in 1968. This typically simple quartz-watch (1985) was designed by two architects. Everything visible is made from stainless steel, and the ultra-thin case and bracelet have been polished with diamond dust.

journey to your collection. If you cannot attend the auction, you can leave a written bid (always remember the buyers' premium!) free of charge, but note that where identical bids are left for the same lot the earliest one lodged gains the lot. Auctioneers are sensible enough not to accept written instructions which state 'no upper limit'!

Sales at auctions attract deductions from the sellers' final cheques (which arrives between 14 and 35 days later, depending on the auction house, and only after the buyer has paid). Commissions on hammer prices obtained generally range from 10% to 15% (plus VAT), with minimum payments of between £20 and £50 per lot. In addition sellers may have to pay obligatory insurance, and previously agreed photography and freight costs. Finally, express sales (which not all auctioneers feature) and unbought lots with sellers' reserves may also attract deductions from those cheques.

An auction of watches and clocks in progress at Christie's King Street salerooms in London. The 9-carat gold Rolex Prince, dated 1936, shown as Lot 240, fetched £3,680, including the buyer's premium. The pre-sale estimate was £2,500-3,000.

COLLECTABLE
WRISTWATCHES

Two very similar models in René Boivin's range of fashion watches. The bezels have mobile sections over them set with precious stones, which can enclose or reveal jewelled settings beneath. The dials are in natural mother of pearl.

AUDEMARS PIGUET

Audemars Piguet's Royal Oak automatic was launched in 1972, and has been available in various combinations of metals ever since. It is notable for its eight highly visible screws; the bezels on both the ladies' (left) and gentlemen's dress watches in 18-carat gold are set with brilliants.

Ever since Jules Audemars met Edouard Piguet in Le Brassus, one of the great Swiss watchmaking towns, in 1875 some of the world's finest watches have appeared. 'AP' watches have always been expensive, and yet are highly collectable because they are not mass-produced and are all manufactured under one roof. Every one of their watches bears a different number which is recorded in Le Brassus for all time.

The firm has never ceased bringing out innovative models. In 1946 'AP' produced the then thinnest wristwatch ever made (1.64 mm). The steel and gold Royal Oak has been popular since 1972, with its ship's porthole appearance. Their first automatic perpetual calendar watch came six years later; it does not need adjustment for leap years until 2100! The firm makes only up to 15,000 watches a year, and they range from plain dial automatics to mixed gold jewel-encrusted chronographs with moon phases and three subsidiary dials. Yet some models remain towards the lower end of the [B] band. For example there is a tonneau-shaped early 1970s 18-carat white gold wristwatch with an associated 18-carat white gold bracelet. The crisply elegant dial has black roman numerals and black baton hands on a matt silvered dial, but no seconds hands. Further up the [B] bracket a round 1968 18-carat ultra-thin watch with a flat band-like bezel will appeal to chasers after ultimate simplicity in their timepieces. This is reinforced by much extended thin black baton numerals and thin gold baton hands.

The ultra-thin automatic with the date window on the left was launched by Audemars Piguet in 1969. It was a platinum version of the 1946 model on the right. Both have transparent case backs, and are fine examples of this maker's achievements in classic simplicity.

BAUME & MERCIER

Baume & Mercier's Riviera in stainless steel has an integrated bracelet. The date window is placed neatly at 6 o'clock.

William Baume, of the Geneva clockmaking family in business since 1830, met Paul Tchereditchenko in 1912. The latter was the son of a Czarist officer and an embroideress with Worth, the couturier. Fortunately he had changed his name to the more euphonic Mercier by the time they joined up in business in 1918.

That family connection with Worth was soon reflected in Baume & Mercier's ladies' fashion watches, with fancy case shapes, jewelled bezels and highly ornate bracelets; they were exquisitely dainty, and are well worth looking out for. They are about, because Baume Bros. was set up as an importer in England in the late 19th century, and the wristwatches to follow were vigorously marketed. The Greek letter PHI was adopted as a dial logo in the mid-1960s. It evokes Vitruvius's Golden Section; Leonardo da Vinci renamed it Divine Proportion, and indeed today Baume & Mercier formal watches have a classical, clean, elegant look about them. Their production numbers are high and retail prices on the low side, but collectors do have particular models to look out for. One is the 18-carat gold oval ladies' International, from 1968-69, with a flexible, braided gold bracelet [B]. A more recent classic B & M watch is the sports Riviera, with its 12-sided bezel.

On the dial of this elegant quartz 18-carat yellow gold Baume & Mercier watch all the markings and hands have the same visual weight values.

BLANCPAIN

This classically simple Blancpain is automatic and in rose gold. It has a 'see-through' sapphire back.

Blancpain has been producing distinctive watches since 1815 and is famous for its statement that it will never make a quartz wristwatch. One of its most famous innovations was an automatic or self-winding mechanism in 1926 (invented by an Englishman, John Harwood). 'Rayville' appeared on Blancpain watch dials from about 1932 for some 40 years; the name is a phonetic reversal of Villeret, where Blancpain was then located. Between 1970 and 1983 there was no production. Now some 7000 watches a year flow again from Le Brassus, and each one is entered with its number in a register. A genuine Blancpain can always be verified.

The simple white dials of these watches are renowned for their uncluttered displays of the time, and for their ultra-thin models. A Blancpain minute repeater (of which only about ten are made each year) should be in any collection with a substantial budget. It can repeat, via a lever on its side, the hour, quarter hour and minute in chimes, whilst the main movement continues. Blancpain has successfully completed the other five great achievements in wristwatch manufacture: chronometer, moonphase calendar, perpetual calendar, tourbillon regulator, and ultra-thin chronograph. In 1993 Blancpain, which had changed ownership the previous year, surprised the horological world by launching a unique series of erotic watches (known in the trade as 'bonking' watches). These 18-carat gold models have mechanical movements (of course) and only a single watch of each design (based on paintings by the French 18th-century artist François Boucher) will ever be made. Cost? £89,950 each, if you can ever lay your hands on one.

Blancpain's top-of-the-range Tourbillon model in 18-carat rose gold.

BREGUET

This Breguet, for the French market, has day and date windows and a moonphase indicator. It naturally has so-called Breguet hands (which date from 1800), and the watch number is unique to it.

This is probably the most famous single name in watchmaking history. Swiss-born Abraham-Louis Breguet (1747-1823) developed in Paris the first automatic watch (the perpetuelle, as he called it) in about 1783. Hour and minute hands with small round holes before the points are still called Breguet hands in honour of his original design. He also invented the perpetual calendar and the tourbillon movement. Today's Breguet wristwatches still feature his distinctive engine-turned dials, and most of them also display their unique serial numbers, which are quite as valuable as classic car chassis numbers to collectors.

One unusually attractive feature of many dials of Breguet automatic wristwatches is a fan-shaped power reserve indicator. In about 1932 this wonderful maker produced a rectangular platinum watch with such an indicator below 12 o'clock on the familiar engine-turned silvered dial. Below the central hands, over 6 o'clock sat a seconds and calendar subsidiary dial; the watch's symmetry is completed by the crown above 12 o'clock. In the 1920s and 1930s Breguet was naturally tuned in to the very latest Parisian fashion styles, and so their jewelled ladies' (generally rectangular) watches in Art Nouveau and Art Deco designs are often on collectors' short lists of desirable mechanicals. The full remarkable story of Abraham-Louis Breguet and his creations is told in 'The Art of Breguet' by the great British watchmaker George Daniels (Sotheby's/Philip Wilson Publishers).

This watch has a Messidor tourbillon movement which is partly visible on the silvered engine-turned dial, and totally from the back. The dial bears Breguet's secret signature.

BREITLING

This is a ladies' Breitling wristwatch. The Callistino II has an automatic mechanical movement, and comes in various combinations of metals. It has Breitling accessories such as a ratcheted, unidirectional rotating bezel, and a screw-locked crown.

The Breitling image is that of the great outdoors, sport and technical achievement. The Grenchen company was founded in 1884 by Léon Breitling in St Imier and started manufacturing wristwatches in 1914 to meet wartime demands. Introduced by Léon's son Gaston Breitling they had luminous dials and a stopwatch mechanism, for use in the trenches. Between the wars cockpit watches were produced by grandson Willy Breitling for American aeroplane makers, and in 1952 came the renowned Navitimer. This pilot's chronograph is preferred by collectors to its quartz successor, the Cosmonaute (1962). The Navitimer GMT was introduced in 1983 (four years after Ernest Schneider acquired the company); it shows three time zones simultaneously (two analogue and one digital), and has separate power sources for two movements as a safety factor. This pilot's chronograph is also water-resistant! The quartz version was to come in 1983.

In 1958 came the Superocean, with a water-resistant one piece case. Another 'first' was the 1967 Chronoslide sports and industrial chronometer, which features a circular slide rule. Another collectable sporting watch is the 1970 Breitling GMT. This chronograph has two hour hands, one addressing a 12-hour face, the other a 24-hour one. Finally, for the wealthy yet intrepid the Breitling Emergency has a built-in antenna which can activate a water-resistant transmitter for broadcasting emergency signals for up to 28 days continuously, over between 5 and 20 kilometres, depending on the terrain. All these watches are expensive if their condition is very good [B~D], but there are plenty of less expensive handsome mid-1930s steel complicated Breitlings in the [A] bracket; the 1934ish Montbrillant range for example.

In 1993 Breitling introduced this Old Navitimer QP chrono-graph. It is a replica of the classic 1952 Navitimer, with added perpetual calendar and moonphases. It is available in white or pink 18-carat gold.

BULOVA

*Fashion watches by Bulova for 'United Colors of Benetton'.
Chictime is on the left. The automatic 'Time of the World:
Ecology Performance' watch on the right is seen from the back.
The crown is unusually on the left.*

Original American Bulova watches have always
attracted collectors. It is most famous of course for the
Accutron (1960; production ended in 1976), the electronic tuning fork watch invented by Max Hetzel.
Different models include the skeletonized Spaceview
(1963), the officially approved Railroad (1963), the
Astronaut (c.1970), and the oval Accutron Date
(c.1975) with its raised chapter ring. The basic cushion-shaped skeleton Accutron belongs in any general
collection. All these watches should be in price band
[A].

Bulova is also noted for its range of ladies' Excel-
lency wristwatches. These late 1920s models are
highly decorative, with handmade rectangular cases
often encrusted with precious stones [B]. Less expensive, but none the less appealing, are some delicate
oval ladies' watches from the late 1960s, such as
Concerto, First Lady, Lady Bulova, and La Petite. For
men, among collectable Bulova watches is the Lone
Eagle (1927), produced in honour of Charles

Lindbergh's first solo non-stop trans-Atlantic flight in 1927. Its rectangular white rolled gold case encloses raised gold hands and numerals [A]. The curved tonneau case of Bulova's Minuteman is handsome [A], and so are the 1935 Phantom [A] and the 1941 Montgomery [A]. The self-winding Commander (c.1966) also has appeal if in very good condition; both 1966 versions had luminous dials.

The Bulova Accutron was introduced in 1960 as the world's first electronic tuning fork watch. Man first landed on the moon in July 1969, and placed an Accutron ultra-accurate timing device on its surface, where it remains today. Above is the Spaceview model.

CARTIER

One of Cartier's classic wristwatch ranges, the Santos, first manufactured privately in 1904 for a Brazilian balloonist, Alberto Santos-Dumont, who was a friend of Louis-François Cartier. The Santos went on general sale in 1911. This 18-carat gold automatic is the Santos Ronde.

The history of this world-famous company goes back to Louis-François Cartier (1819-1904) who took over the jewellery workshop of Adolphe Picard in Paris in 1847. His son and successor Louis Cartier greatly expanded the enterprise. The luxury brand name of Cartier has long been associated with wristwatches. After producing a few ladies' fashion wristwatches with gold and diamond bracelets (with remarkable prescience) between 1888 and 1894, Cartier reached a wide market for the first time with its Santos Dumont (1911), which is still made today. It is named after a Brazilian balloonist and early aviator, who specially commissioned it.

Other famous pre-1914 models included the Tonneau (1906), Baignoire (1912) and Tortue (1912). The world-famous Cartier Tank watch was launched in 1919; the austere simplicity of its case shape (inspired by twin tank tracks longer than the fighting machine between them) has never lost its appeal for collectors; you could spend half a lifetime gathering one each of the different Cartier Tank dial designs. Other models to look out for in the sale rooms today are the Pasha (1932), which was the first luxury water-resistant wristwatch, and the Vendôme (1933), with its single lugs. The Calandre, in the shape of a riding stirrup, was another notable design, with its asymmetric lugs. Cartier wristwatches have always been made in a great variety of shapes, perhaps because the company is a retailer as well and has always understood the vagaries of customer taste. In recent years the Must de Cartier lines have gained a following – a brand within a brand.

A Cartier Pasha, first produced in 1932 for the Pasha of Morocco for use in his swimming pool.

CERTINA

This modern Certina gentlemen's watch has a mechanical movement, is gold plated with a silvered dial, and also bears the name of the founding brothers.

Certina started its business existence as Kurth Frères in 1888 in the Swiss town of Grenchen. Adolf and Alfred Kurth used several brand names for their prize-winning pocket watches and later wristwatches, the best known of which were Grana and Narzisse. Particularly notable was the square 18-carat gold Curvex Hunter, with arabic numerals on a black enamel dial and a square subsidiary seconds dial at 6 o'clock [B]. Simple square-case Granas in 14-carat gold with similar dials are less expensive.

The name Certina (certus is Latin for reliable) was adopted in 1948. The 1968 Certina Free Form was a highly unusual design. The octagonal case, with its mother-of-pearl dial and baton numerals, had the crown at 12 o'clock and was set within a rectangular outer frame which also acted as lugs [A]. The 1950s 14-carat gold King and Queen, with their majestic lugs and squared-off dials and dauphine hands, make fine collectors' pieces (the ladies' model has no subsidiary seconds dial) [A]. Distinctive ladies' models of the period include the Flair, Debutante and Olivia. On all these the lugwork is most original in design. The 1958 DS (which stands for Double Security) is a classic, with its unique 'floating' movement bed; recently a new generation of DS wristwatches has been launched.

This very attractive watch from Certina is the Biostar Electronic. The 1960s image lies in the case shape and the three biorhythm readings between the markers in the main aperture. The date aperture is at 3 o'clock.

CHOPARD

This 18-carat yellow gold perpetual calendar chronograph by Chopard has an automatic movement.

Louis-Ulysse Chopard founded this business in 1860 in Sonvillier in the Swiss Jura mountains, and became a large supplier of pocket watches to the Swiss railways. In 1920 the factory was moved to Meyrin-Genève, where, much expanded, it remains today. In 1963 the Scheufele family acquired the company; it had been making jewellery and jewelled watches in Pforzheim, in Germany, since 1904.

The 1976 Happy Diamonds wristwatch, designed by Roland Kurowski, with diamonds moving freely and visibly around inside the bezel and all around the plain, unnumbered dial, is an expensive acquired taste but certainly original [E]. Chopard's first-ever sports watch was the 1980 St Moritz and displays eight distinctly functional screws which connect the case and bezel. The 1988 Mille Miglia (in 18-carat gold or

gold and steel) chronograph commemorates the re-
starting of the famous road sports-car race from
Brescia to Rome and back; naturally it incorporates a
tachymetre and luminous hands and baton numerals
[B]. Chopard's perpetual calendar chronograph was
produced in a limited edition of 150 – fifty each in
yellow gold, pink gold and platinum. Chopard's jewelled watches are sought after by some lady collectors
for their unusual shapes as well as stone settings...ovals,
diamonds, baguettes, and sometimes with no visible
lugs [generally B].

*Chopard introduced its Happy Diamonds watch concept in
1976. This ladies' quartz piece is in yellow gold.*

CITIZEN

The mass of information on this Citizen world timer is offset by the outline world map behind the four subsidiary dials.

The Japanese Citizen Watch Company was founded in 1930, and exports commenced six years later to the Pacific Rim which it was later to dominate. In 1953 Citizen acquired the Rhythm Watch Company, and in the next few years exported its manufacturing techniques to India in a big way. The famous typographic Citizen logo was fully established in 1970.

The recent history of Citizen is full of 'firsts' as it grew to become a dominant force in world watchmaking, and a leader in the invasion of Switzerland's very long-established market in mechanical wristwatches in the mid and late 1970s and early 1980s. 1973 saw the launch of its analogue Quartz Cryston. There then followed the Mega-Quartz (1975; with an accuracy of three seconds a year), Quartz Cryston Solar Cell (1976; the first quartz LCD watch using sunlight as a power source), the Citizen Quartz 790 (1978; an ultra-thin analogue quartz less than 1mm thick), the Aqualand (1985; the first diver's watch with an electronic depth meter), the Altichron (1989; the first climber's watch with an elevation sensor), the Citizen Quartz Perpetual Calendar (1989; the first quartz watch to incorporate a 200-year-long calendar, accounting for future leap year irregularities), the Citizen Analogue Quartz Minute Repeater (1991; with free time signal, local time display and multi-alarm functions). Endless future horological innovations can be expected from Citizen.

Citizen's Aqualand gives a diver's depth from 1m to 80m in 0.1 m increments, accurate to 3% of depth indicated. It 'beeps' when a preset depth has been reached. It is water-resistant to 200m. Models with feet measurements are also available.

CONCORD

The Concord Saratoga is in 18-carat gold with an integrated bracelet, the cost of which enhances the value of the whole. The quartz movement is ultra-thin.

Soon after its foundation in 1908 in Bienne, Concord was experimenting with the manufacture of ultra-thin pocket watches – to slip easily into the waistcoats so widely worn in those days. In 1914 the Swiss army adopted Concord wristwatches made in stainless steel. The 1920s Eight Day watch, which required winding only once a week, became very popular as the habit of travelling grew.

The tradition of Concord's quest for thinness continued, and was to result in the production in 1979 of what was then the thinnest wristwatch in the world – a mere 1.98mm thick. This quartz watch, the Concord Delirium, now belongs in any collection of innovatory models. One successor, the Delirium IV, was just 0.98mm thick – but not suitable for normal wearing. This 1981 wristwatch was issued in a limited edition and is also a collector's item. Today's Deliriums, with or without jewelled bezels and integrated bracelets, and with plain unnumbered round dials within rectangular cases, in 18-carat gold in both ladies' and gentlemen's sizes, frequently appear in sale rooms [B]. They display a distinctive feature of Concord wristwatches: uncluttered dials, no subsidiary dials, and a single baton marker at 12 o'clock. Other Concord quartz watches have a full set of baton hour markers.

This 18-carat yellow gold Delirium is a typical Concord wristwatch, and is enclosed in a brushed stainless steel case.

CORUM

These 18-carat gold ladies' watches were created by Corum in 1958. Chapeau Chinois is on the left; the other is the Oeil.

This Swiss family company was founded in La Chaux-de-Fonds in 1924 by Gaston Ries, and incorporated as Corum in 1955, when his daughter Simone and nephew René Bannwart became partners. It has produced some established classic wristwatches which appeal to collectors, and often fetch good prices at auction. Its quartz Coin watch (1965), for example, has an ultra-thin movement enclosed between two halves of a genuine US 20 dollar 'Double Eagle' gold coin. The Ingot watches (1977) incorporated 99.99% pure gold ingots, in various weights, and their assay certificates ensured minimum market values.

The Romulus watch (1966) was the first-ever to feature hour markers in roman numerals on the gold or platinum bezel instead of the dial. In Corum's Platinum range there is a handsome square-cased curvex model with French numerals spelt out on the dial. Car watch collectors should look out for the 1976

Rolls-Royce watch; the Spirit of Ecstasy bonnet mascot is set within the top lug. Another Corum original comes in a limited edition of 999 – for a good reason! The dial on the Météorite (1986) is made up of slices of the Cape York meteorite which had fallen on Greenland. Collectors will note that the material is unique (unlike, say, gold) and no two dials can possibly be the same in design. Although more recent watches, such as Admiral's Cup (1983), are successes, some earlier ones really catch the eye. The 1965 Buckingham was a curved outsized watch in a choice of metals. Square in shape with a very original arrangement of horizontal baton numerals, its simplicity is emphasised by the absence of a seconds hand.

Corum's Buckingham (1965). This large gentlemen's mechanical model features the hours spelt out in French, and, at 9 o'clock, the initials of Jean-René Bannwart. Since 1978 an attractive platinum version has been available.

CYMA

The black dial and leather strap nicely set off the yellow gold case of this quartz Banane from Cyma.

Today a maker of elegant quartz timepieces based in Le Locle, this privately owned company was founded in 1862 in a small village in Switzerland's Jura mountains. As early as 1891 it was making complicated repeater movements for its pocket watches, and by 1903 the company was producing very thin lever movements.

In the late 1920s Cyma was turning out quality timepieces in great quantities which today are firmly in the [A] price band. Many of them had a subsidiary seconds dial which unusually did not completely cover the 6 o'clock numeral, and most models had detachable lugs. It would be fair to call this output 'pretty little watches' of no great distinction. Hefty arabic numerals were generally in radium (which is not permissible today). Early 1920s ladies' wristwatches were usually round, in a choice of metals, with dainty engravings around the cases. One gentlemen's model of the period had elongated roman numerals which extended back to the bezel on an 18-carat gold case. In 1988 Cyma introduced Le Double D'Or. This fine technical achievement has two quartz movements; the top one, which is hinged for opening, has an unnumbered dial and baton hands, while beneath there is a traditional dial with roman hour markers and a seconds chapter ring [B].

Cyma's Golden Duo wristwatch which is two watches in one case. The top dial is modern while the lower has a traditional appearance.

DUNHILL

The square 1936 Dunhill 18-carat gold watch, with eccentric raised arabic numerals, is another Dunhill collectable. Its case shape is somewhat reminiscent of Cartier's Santos.

This famous luxury goods and tobacco company celebrated its centenary in 1993 by producing six models of an attractive 18-carat gold wristwatch, called Centenary, in a limited edition of 100. The company's first signed watch, a double-sided tachymetre for car dashboards, appeared in 1906. Its famous watch lighters came in 1926, and three years later it produced the La Captive pocket watch and the silver Dunhill Belt Watch. In 1929 the first Dunhill wristwatch was launched. This desirable timepiece, which is very rare, is rectangular with exotic sloping arabic numerals within a pierced border. The gold case is numbered on the lower front side.

Alfred Dunhill launched their first ladies' wristwatches in 1936, and these are sought after because they were very fashionable presents at the time. Through the years single lugs have been a constant feature in Dunhill watch ranges. Single flat lugs are a feature of the 1975 Vermeil, which is round, with the company's logo on a gold machined dial, big roman numerals and black baton hands, and a cabochon on the crown. The Millennium range, with 30 different models, was launched in 1982 and also has the single lugs. The Dunhill Limited Edition Dress Watch, with its sapphire back plate, deserves consideration.

This 18-carat octagonal wristwatch is dated 1925, and is the first one known to be signed by Dunhill. The luxury goods company was founded in 1893.

EBEL

Ebel's 18-carat gold automatic chronograph with perpetual calendar. The crown is protected and the watch is water-resistant to 100 ft (30 m).

Eugène Blum founded a watch factory in 1911 in La Chaux-de-Fonds, and it took its unusual name from the initial letters of 'Eugène Blum Et Lévy' (the latter was his wife's maiden name). The firm of Ebel was originally just an assembler of watches, from parts made by small family companies throughout Switzerland's Vallée de Joux. Charles Blum succeeded his father, and until early in 1994 his grandson Pierre-Alain owned it. The first real Ebel-made watch was the Sports model (1977). The Beluga range followed in 1985. In both lines the dials, bezels, straps and bracelets are interchangeable, and they come in various sizes. This means that, theoretically, a huge number of different Ebel models are around.

There is now a perpetual calendar chronograph in the Sports and Beluga ranges, incorporating the familiar Ebel screws on the case fronts. The bracelets, which Ebel also make themselves, are a distinctive feature of these timepieces. They are often wholly integrated with the cases, and generally consist of 190 or more separate parts. The 18-carat gold Ebel 1911 offers a fine top of the range example of such integration. This watch marked the firm's 75th anniversary in 1986 and has an unusual domed sapphire crystal. Ebel is famed for its involvement in sports sponsorship, to project its dynamic image; golf, tennis, and athletics and also the music world, have benefited, as have the sales of its range of automatic, mechanical and quartz timepieces.

The conceptual design stage for an Ebel 18-carat gold automatic chronograph. Bracelets are a distinctive and integrated feature of many Ebel wristwatches.

ELGIN

An elegant, rectangular rolled gold Elgin with stepped lug supports.

This famous American maker was founded as the Elgin National Watch Co. in 1867 in Elgin, Illinois. They produced their first ladies' watches in about 1906, but 1928-1931 saw the introduction of literally hundreds of different ladies' models. They were slim, broadly rectangular, with same-sized movements, in sometimes brilliantly original Art Deco designs. They had names like Madame Susie, Madame Agnès, Madame Amy and Madame Jenny – and Madame Alpha III, American Beauty, Style-Line and many wonderful designs by Lucien Lelong. All are price band [A], as they were made in huge quantities.

Gentlemen were catered for as well by Elgin during this time. There was a large range of Clubman, Presentation and Thrift models (all serially numbered). Inevitably, up-market Lord Elgin wristwatches were made [A; sometimes B]. Towards the end of the First World War Elgin produced a military wristwatch; this had a pierced case, luminous arabic numerals and hands, for night use, and a strong khaki strap [A]. During the Second World War Elgin made the steel Navigation Hack Watch for the American Army Air Corps, and also a Marine Corps Watch [both A]. Its c.1940 U.S. Navy diver's watch had a screwed-down case and a hugely oversized crown [A]. In all Elgin made over 50 million movements, and they are not rare. Worth looking out though is a 1930s cushion-shaped gentlemen's chronometer, with roman numerals on a black enamelled bezel.

Lord Elgin wristwatches were first introduced in 1937. The arrangement of semi-precious stones on the dial of this model give it a distinctive appearance.

ETERNA

Eterna's 1856 collection derives from the Eterna-Matic, launched in 1948. Case shapes now available are square, round, tonneau and oval. For this round version there is a choice of mechanical, automatic or quartz movements.

In 1856, in the small Jura mountain town of Grenchen, Josef Girard, a doctor, and Anton Schild established a watch apprentices' workshop. Anton's son Urs set up a watch production line in 1870 to produce ébauches. Complete pocket watches came in 1876, branded Eterna. First Anton's grandson Max and then his brother Theodor helped develop the business, and in 1906 it was incorporated as Fabriques Eterna, Schild Frères & Co.

The first alarm wristwatch from Eterna, round, with bold sans-serif arabic numerals, was introduced in 1914 with a protective metal grille for military use. Ladies' unusually small baguette-shaped wristwatches were very successful in the 1930s, whilst the original ébauches business, by then called ETA, flourished (as a subsidiary of Ebauches S.A., set up in 1926). The sought-after self-winding Eterna-Matic, with its five-dot logo (the company's symbol ever since) appeared in 1948, with only the even numerals stated. The first ladies' version came in 1952. The Golden Eterna-Matic of the 1950s, with dagger hands and sweep seconds within a simple round case and within prominent curved lugs, is a nicely understated collectors' piece. Gina Lollobrigida's advertising helped make the ladies' Eterna's Golden Heart (1958) extremely popular. In the same year the KonTiki water-resistant watch was launched.

This ladies' Eterna, with its strikingly coloured bracelet, retains the simple dial presentation which is typical of this maker.

FORTIS

Fortis introduced the Hedonist Business quartz watch in 1991. The range was the first Swiss watch to display 52 calendar weeks, and was offered with either automatic or mechanical movements.

Fortis was established by Walter Vogt in the Swiss town of Grenchen in 1912, and from the beginning he was looking for sales abroad. His watches were modest little mechanicals, generally rectangular with silvered dials in 14-carat gold [A]; they were distributed throughout the United States from New York. This eye for export markets brought him a meeting, in Switzerland, with the English watch inventor John Harwood who, in 1924, had patented in both England and Switzerland a self-winding watch. This 'world-first' maintained its power by its wearers' movements. Fortis brought out its first Harwood watch in 1926, and has been selling versions almost ever since (see the separate account of Harwood).

Another true Fortis innovation was the first plastic-cased watch, the Flipper, in 1968. Their extremely colourful totally informal designs enclosed 'container systems' by which bezels and straps were interchangeable, and which incorporated quartz analogue date movements. The world of show business immediately recognized the fun and use of the Flipper, and soon it was being sported by stars such as Mick Jagger, Jerry Hall, Michael Caine, Liza Minnelli and Rod Stewart. The early ones are collectable and long pre-date Swatches. Well worth looking out for as well is the 1930s Rolls and Autorist. Fortis do of course have a fine range of more traditional pieces, such as the Hedonist and the 1962 Stratoliner.

The Flipper range of watches was launched by Fortis in 1968, anticipating both its own Logo Swiss collection and the Swatches.

GIRARD-PERREGAUX

Girard-Perregaux's Equation Espace was launched in 1985. A year is travelled by the small golden ball within the concentric rings, indicating the seasons, months, solstices and equinoxes as they occur. The movement is a combination of electronic quartz and micromechanics. It was originated by Francis P.-A. Besson.

This is one of the great old names in Swiss watch-making, and will always be known for the fact that it produced the world's first mass-produced wristwatch – in 1880. It was for German naval officers, and its dial had a protective metal grille. This is a classic collec-tors' piece. The company was founded in 1791 and acquired its present name in 1856.

From the beginning it produced fine pocket watches, of which the most famous is the Tourbillon With Three Golden Bridges, a gold hunter, in the early 1850s. It used Breguet's tourbillon. Innovation has long been a watchword at Girard-Perregaux, and in 1969 it set up the first Swiss production line for quartz watches (the selected oscillation of 32,768 Hz is now standard). It was thus well placed to withstand the Japanese quartz invasion in the world's markets in the early 1970s. A highly distinctive range to look out for is the Equation, which includes the Equation Focale, with its peaked sapphire within a wide flat circular bezel, with the date at 12 o'clock. The Equation Espace Perpétuelle gives the days, seasons, leap years (with the variations), moonphases, solstices, equinoxes and zodiac sign periods. A most collectable package!

The world's first known mass-produced wristwatch, produced from 1880 for German naval officers by Girard-Perregaux. A great prize for any collection!

GRUEN

The jewelled lugs on this rectangular Gruen Precision watch indicate an early 1930s date.

Gruen did not start producing wristwatches in any great quantity until 1910 (for ladies) and 1918 (for men); it had been founded back in 1874 in Columbus, Ohio. In 1910 it had joined in the market which Elgin was already successfully supplying – inexpensive highly decorative ladies' wristlet watches. It also, however, featured watches in platinum, set with diamonds; the Fifth Avenue and Park Avenue came in a variety of diamond colours and sizes [both B]. The 1950 clover-shaped Henrietta in 14-carat gold is highly unusual.

The early 1930s rectangular gentlemen's Quadrons are noteworthy. 1937 saw Gruen's famous Curvex Majesty and Curvex Patroness in extra long 14-carat rolled gold sharply curved cases [A]; these led to smaller Curvex models around 1940. Collectors keen on the 1940s look out for Gruen's duo-dial Doctor's

Watches, with raised gold arabic numerals in both the hour and minute and the smaller seconds dial [A]. Soon after the Second World War the company produced the triple faceted Curvex and Executive, both with single diamonds as hour markers at 9, 12 and 3 o'clock; the large curved cases came in a choice of 14-carat yellow, white or pink gold [B]. Wristwatch collections based on originality would be well adorned by Gruen's remarkable Day-Nite from the mid-1960s. The baton hour markers change colour at 6 pm to a fluorescent glow, and they stay that way until 6 am.

This Gruen Precision Auto-Wind is dated at about 1965. The bezel and hour marker designs give this rolled gold wristwatch a highly distinctive look.

HAMILTON

This modern Hamilton automatic, the Odyssee 2001, has a case design which recalls the unique range of this maker's late 1950s and 1960s models. The recessed crown preserves the circular shape. Note the different lug treatments.

This is the most notable name among American watchmakers (of which there is not one left today). It was established in Lancaster, Pennsylvania in 1892 to make pocket watches. As so frequently it was wartime demand that led to the first Hamilton wristwatches in late 1914.

Today the company is best remembered for its 'electric' wristwatches. The Hamilton 505 was introduced in 1958 as the world's first electric watch. In fact Hamilton, Elgin and Lip (France) first brought out somewhat primitive electric watches in 1952; Epperlein (Germany) and Landeron (Switzerland) followed them. The most prominent of its virtues was that it never needed winding, whether worn or stored, for up to two years – after which its energy cell needed replacement. Its electric movement never required adjustment, was antimagnetic and shock resistant. It was soon appearing in a huge selection of models, and the most collectable are those with highly unusual case shapes and dial designs. Prices range from [A] for end-of-the-range Grade 500 such as the Sea-Lectric-1, Everest Electric (with its arabic 12 on the upper lug, 1958), Victor Electric and Titan Electric, to middle [B] for the distinctive Ventura Electric (c.1958). Each Electric watch has that word on the dial. In 1963 the Thin-O-Matic [A] was launched. From about 1964 Hamilton produced a line of gentlemen's watches with diamonds for hour markers; one each of the Lord Lancaster watches [A, B, C, etc.] would make a fine, if flashy, collection. Finally, the Hamilton Computer Pulsar is on most shortlists of notable American wristwatches. Hamilton closed its American manufacturing company in the 1970s, but the name lives on as a Swiss brand (within the SMH Group) with emphasis on its American origins.

The idiosyncratic shape of this late 1950s Hamilton Ventura Electric has made it an instantly recognisable classic wristwatch.

HARWOOD

A contemporary version of Harwood's pioneering Automatic from 1926. Every Automatic carries a unique registration number.

It is said that John Harwood hit upon the idea for his self-winding movement after watching children playing on a seesaw. That conception in 1923, which he patented the next year, was a truly original one. He then went to Switzerland to identify a manufacturer, and licensed Fortis to manufacture watches incorporating his new mechanism (from which Blancpain developed one prototype only, and also made for the French market). Soon the Harwood Self-Winding Watch Co. Ltd. was in business in London, selling the round, bevelled-edged watch which had no crown at all [B]. Its hands were, as today in modern versions, set by rotating the fluted bezel. The matt white dial featured arabic numerals, with Breguet hour and minute hands, and a dot surrounded by a diamond pattern, just above 6 o'clock; if the dot is red the watch is in a working mode.

The Harwood Watch Co. is today relaunched as a Grenchen watchmaker. After its success with Harwood's Automatic (1926), Fortis maintained its close contact with John Harwood. In 1931 it produced the Autorist [B], Harwood's next invention. This sought-after watch was powered by the wearer's movement of the bracelet which had a special attachment to the side of the watch.

Lady Hay timing the Flight of the Graf Zeppelin with a Harwood Self-Winding Watch.

The massive Graf Zeppelin was launched in September 1928 and flew over one million miles in 590 flights up to 1937. Lady Hay was a journalist on one of its global flights. It also crossed the Atlantic 144 times.

INGERSOLL

'Tell the time at night - with Radiolite' ran the old jingle promoting this quartz Ingersoll watch. The push-button at 4 o'clock activates the dial illumination.

'The watch that made the dollar famous' was Ingersoll's Yankee pocket watch which was launched in New York in 1895. That low retail price, together with a year's guarantee and vigorous, original marketing ploys, soon made the Michigan-born Ingersoll brothers both famous and rich. Their first wristwatch came in 1913, with a luminous dial. In 1930 Ingersoll Ltd was formed in Britain, and soon watches were flowing out of Clerkenwell.

In 1933 Ingersoll produced the first of a long line of 'character' watches; it was the Mickey Mouse and remains the best-known and sought after (actually it was first made for Disney in 1928 to promote the new cartoon). These watches, made mostly with dials of printed cardboard, are always prominent in bargain boxes in street market and car boot sales. There are guides to them, and the watches to go for are the earliest ones, in mint condition (which is rare) and featuring the best-known characters. The peak of Ingersoll's British production was in the 1950s and 1960s, when they were made by the million. (Today no wristwatches are made in Great Britain.) Ingersoll's plain, round, steel chronometers were for a long time given to children as their first watches [low A]. Their names, such as Midget and Mite, therefore live on, as do 'occupation' watches, such as Engineer, Ballerina and Junior Nurse.

Ingersoll's 55 range of quartz wristwatches are boxed in tins with typical 1950s illustrations. They each carry a famous advertising byline.

INTERNATIONAL WATCH COMPANY

IWC takes 18 months to make each Da Vinci. This 18-carat gold automatic chronograph with perpetual calendar and moonphase indicator was the first wristwatch to feature a year window.

IWC, as it is conveniently known, had to struggle hard to survive in the 1870s, with Swiss-made pocket watches intended for America by its American co-founders. But its strong practical wristwatches sold widely during the First World War, with their luminous dials. C.G.Jung, the Swiss psychiatrist, gladly received dividends from family shares in IWC at that time!

A classic wristwatch for collectors was launched by IWC in 1940. The Fliegerchronograph (pilot's watch with stop mechanism) has luminous sans-serif arabic numbers on a large black dial, with a sweep seconds hand. It had an inner case of 'soft iron' which protected the movement from magnetic fields, and its extra long strap meant it would go on top of a thick flying jacket. The Ingenieur watches (1946) have always attracted technically minded collectors because of their complicated multi-function movements.

IWC's first quartz movements went into the Da Vinci range (1969); its tuning forks give a very faint 'whistling' sound. The International Watch Company commissioned Ferdinand Porsche (of car fame) to design a watch for them, and his Compass watch (1978) was a trendsetter. It can also be used as a pocket compass.

The case of this Da Vinci from IWC is made from zirconium oxide (which is originally white) in a very long manufacturing process. The final stage is the polishing of the fired blank.

JAEGER-LECOULTRE

The automatic moonphase model in Jaeger-LeCoultre's Odysseus range. The case is in 18-carat yellow gold. The seconds hand design alludes to the lunar function.

Antoine LeCoultre opened a watch movement workshop in 1833 in Le Sentier, Switzerland. It was his grandson, Jacques-David, who merged the business with that of Edmund Jaeger in 1937, to produce today's famous name. The root cause for that combination lay in the story of Jaeger-LeCoultre's sought-after Reverso watch. Swiss-born César de Trey was a gold denture maker in England in the 1920s. While visiting British Army offices in India in 1930 he heard constant complaints from polo players having their wristwatches smashed – and an idea was born. Back in the Vallée de Joux, Switzerland, he discussed it with Jacques-David LeCoultre, who took it to his friend Edmund Jaeger in Paris. The designer and engineer René-Alfred Chauvot filed a patent application in March 1931 for his solution to the polo players' problem – a watch that could be 'slid in its support and completely turned over'.

Until 1937 dials had 'Reverso' alone, or 'Reverso Jaeger' (French), or 'Reverso LeCoultre' (Swiss). Throughout the late 1930s Reversos were made under licence by the new joint company for Cartier, Gruen, E.Gübelin, Hamilton (then American), Patek Philippe and Türler. Every Reverso bears a unique number on its bottom plate giving the exact date of its manufacture. Another collectable 'first' was the 1956 Memovox, the first automatic wristwatch fitted with an alarm. When the multifunctional Odysseus Perpetual Calendar appeared in 1987 it was the smallest watch of its kind in the world.

The bold case design of this Jaeger-LeCoultre moonphase watch will appeal to collectors who appreciate the prominent month date ring.

JEAN D'EVE

Jean d'Eve's very distinctive Sectora model, showing hours and minutes only on its 'half-dial'. Note the protruding right lugs.

This company started out in 1888, under Charles Barbezat, as Manufacture d'Horlogerie Barbezat-Baillod in Le Locle, but using the dial name Le Phare. That name became the company's in 1905. Unfortunately the Swiss Army requisitioned the watch factory in 1915 — in order to have uniform trousers made there! After the war Le Phare made complicated watches where pairs of trousers had been stitched, and in 1939 moved to La Chaux-de-Fonds. By 1970 it was Switzerland's second largest maker of chronographs. The Jean d'Eve brand was launched in 1981, and Le Phare Jean d'Eve S.A. was formed in 1984.

Le Phare's Memory watches of the late 1920s are noteworthy. The square and round Le Phare moonphase watches, with day and month windows, produced from La Chaux-de-Fonds during 1930-45 are particularly appealing [B]. Le Phare was one of the handful of exhibitors at the first annual Watch, Clock and Jewellery Fair at Basle (which is very important to this day). The Jean d'Eve brand really took off after

1986, having then replaced Le Phare, and one of its memorable watches is the highly unusual Sectora. Its 'half-dial' offers vertical time reading, and belongs in collections of eccentric watches. The 1988 Samara has a unique quartz movement which, when stimulated by wrist movement, receives energy via a condenser. This generator system is heavily patented – and mostly visible to its wearer!

Jean d'Eve's Samara range was introduced in 1988. It incorporated a revolutionary movement called the Generotor System.

JUNGHANS

The Junghans Mega which was launched in 1991 as the first ever radio-controlled analogue wristwatch. There was also a limited numbered edition of 250 pieces in gold.

The start of the American Civil War in 1861 meant that Erhard Junghans could no longer import straw for his hat factory in Germany's Black Forest. So they turned to clock making. Their American-style mass-produced clocks soon found profitable markets, and his son Arthur rapidly expanded the company. By 1903 the Schramberg-based company claimed to be the world's largest clock manufacturer – and its first wristwatch came as late as 1928.

Junghans' 1969 Astro-Quartz wristwatch blazed a trail which it has followed since – with ever more sophisticated timepieces of great interest to collectors of mechanically innovative models. The Solar 1 wristwatch (1986) led to the 1990 Mega 1, the world's first radio-controlled (digital) wristwatch, and then came an analogue version (1991), a ladies' model (1992), a model with seconds hand and date (1993), and the Mega Solar chronograph (1993), with its six months' energy reserve. The latter watch draws its energy from light and its time by radio waves. It has no batteries, and is accurate, Junghans claim, to within one second in a million years! If the solar-driven lithium cell is exhausted after six months of disuse, fresh exposure to light instantly recalls the correct time.

Junghans produced the Mega Solar in 1993. It is the first radio-controlled solar wristwatch and has a six-month energy reserve.

JUVENIA

Juvenia's 18-carat gold Mystère Squelette has an ultra-thin Piguet mechanical movement in finely chased 14-carat gold.

The old Alsatian family name of Ditisheim studs Swiss horological history. In 1860 Jacques Ditisheim establish a watch company in St Imier, in the Vallée de Joux, which is still one of the great watchmaking centres. Today the company makes its watches in La Chaux-de-Fonds, and they are as distinctive as ever.

The late 1930s and early 1940s brought a succession of small-cased gentlemen's leather-strapped wristwatches in mixed metals with very original and particularly bold, eccentric lug arrangements [A]. The almost triangular 1945 Alcantara [A] and Isabean [B] watches (the latter with subsidiary seconds at its triangle apex at 6 o'clock) have distinction. The 1949-50 Jumper, with its large stirrup lugs, 14-carat gold rectangular case and silvered dial, also does. The originals of the now revived Mystère range, launched in 1947, are worth seeking out. The two concentric inner dials are black, the broad chapter ring is transparent, front and back, while the baton hour and minute hands are in red. The lugs on the round case are strap ones [A]. Other models to look out for, from the late 1950s, include the round steel Gentry which is thin and plain with a black dial and baton numerals [A], and the much more amusing rolled gold Planète, the face of which shows three multi-coloured interacting dials giving the hour, minute and seconds.

This Arithmo, introduced by Juvenia in 1945, is so-named because it incorporated a circular slide rule in the outer rings.

LIP

Lip's quartz Mach 2000 model with its unusual red ball crown and off-centre dial, pictured for an evocative advertisement. This mid-1970s watch was designed by Roger Tallon.

The French town of Besançon, east of Dijon and north-west of La Chaux-de-Fonds in Switzerland, has long been a watchmaking centre. A Mr Lipmann set up his pocket watch factory there in 1860 and soon it was flourishing. In 1900 his son Ernest Lipmann decided to put his brand name, Lip, on dials instead of those of retailers (which was then general practice in many European countries). In the early 1920s assembly line mechanical wristwatches in a large variety of designs appeared, and in great numbers. In 1952 the

French company was the first to patent an electric watch movement, and from then on fresh design innovations seemed to go hand in hand with vicissitudes.

The mid-1970s French student and union riots were once centred on the Lip factory, and it led to bankruptcy – after two decades of forward-looking model designs which collectors today seek out. Designers such as Michel Boyer, Isabelle Hebey, Marc Held and Rudi Meyer contributed, but the star was Roger Tallon, with his Mach 2000 line. These ultra-modern electronics and automatics (1974) included the 5478, with its rectangular grey case, round two-colour dial, red hour hand, white minute hand, thin white sweep seconds hand and a large red ball-shaped crown. Their manufacture had ceased by 1984 when the company moved to Morteau, near the Swiss border, but now production is flowing again. The 1960s and 1970s Lip designs are the equals of the later Swatches.

The multi-function model in the Mach 2000 range from Lip. The case is made from black hardened anodised alloy, and the black strap is rubber.

LONGINES

The TN, a quartz 1993 addition to Longines' Conquest range. Its digital functions are countdown, second time zone, chronograph, alarm and a seconds, month, day and date display - all controlled by rotating the crown. TN stands for Twisted Nematic - a technology allowing the digital functions to appear or disappear.

Like so many of today's surviving watchmakers Longines started (in 1832) as assemblers of locally made parts, in St Imier. The first factory was built on Les Longines (Long Meadows), and from the beginning Longines dedicated itself to timing sports events. Its first wristwatches appeared in about 1910, and, as ever, it was the coming World War which fuelled their market; the early ones had front case lids.

Longines' Conquest range of wristwatches is all about extreme precision. The quartz VHP model is up to ten times more accurate than the average quartz watch, because it handles temperature changes. The GMT model, with its round-the-clock hand and rotating bezel, is the watch for world timer collectors. The antimagnetic Conquest 1000 Oe is another watch for the technically minded. Along with Longines' early LCD (liquid crystal display) digital watches, perhaps the most popular watch is the Lindbergh Hour Angle

(1932), developed after Charles Lindbergh's historic trans-Atlantic flight in 1927, which took 33 hours, 30 minutes and 29.8 seconds. In 1987 a smaller Hour Angle was produced in a limited edition: 100 in 18-carat gold and 1000 in stainless steel. No collection of Aviation watches would be complete without Longines' automatic watch. It has a circular, hinged, stainless steel case with two pairs of simple lugs. The gilt matt dial has black roman numerals (most unusually the IIII is stated as IV), and within them is a 0-180 calibration in arabic numerals. Within the latter is a silvered matt revolving centre calibrated 0-60 around the edge and 1-15 in red inside. The gold bezel is subdivided into 150 degrees, corresponding to the arc of rotation the earth makes per hour [B].

The automatic mechanical movement of this Longines skeleton wristwatch is fully visible within its 18-carat yellow gold case. It is in the Ernest Francillon collection of fourteen 18-carat gold watches produced in 1993 to mark the 125th anniversary of the Longines brand.

MIDO

Mido's quartz Ocean Star series is ever-popular. The greatly extended lugs hold the appropriately wavy-patterned bracelet.

Since its establishment in Bienne in 1918 by Georges Schaeren, Mido has offered a succession of carefully targeted practical timepieces – always water-resistant. A breakthrough came in 1934 with the Multifort. This self-winder was designed to resist very extreme weather and wearer-habit conditions, and was successfully promoted as the first automatic, water-resistant, antimagnetic and shockproof wristwatch.

Mido's 1930 radiator-shaped Bugatti model is now a collectors' classic and expensive piece [E]. Mido launched its Ocean Star series in 1959, and the wave motifs on the bracelets of some early models maintain the theme. There is now a great variety of Ocean Star models, and the early ones have the greatest appeal (most of them have date or day/date windows). They incorporate Mido's Aquadura water-resistant system. A more recent model to look out for is the nicely-understated Ocean Star No.1. Only 1,000 were manufactured for collectors of the Cable watch (1987) with an anchor at 12 o'clock and a twisting cable motif around the bezel [B]. Earlier Mido watches worth noting include the late 1940s 14-carat gold Multi-Centerchrono with one, 12 and 24 hour chapter rings, and tachymetre and telemeter rings [A]. The Split Second chronograph of the same period is appealing in its round stainless steel case [B]. The round 1961 Winnetka Stainless Powerwind has most unusual etched hour markers [A].

The Ocean Star Dataday has a sleek contemporary appearance and incorporates the Aquadura water-resistance system. This case and bracelet are in stainless steel. The Ocean Star line was first introduced in 1959.

MOVADO

An unusual rolled gold Movado chronograph, with a stepped bezel and hinged single lugs, giving this modern piece a period look. The tachymetric scale is within the outstanding arabic numerals, in the company of three subsidiary dials..

Movado's Polyplan watch (1912), with its curved wrist-fitting case, is much sought-after. Movado enthusiasts also hunt down the Curviplan (1931) and Novoplan (1934) models. But the watch they are really after is the early mechanical version of the Museum Watch (1961), designed by Nathan George Horwitt back in 1947. His lone gold dot placed at 12 o'clock represents the sun's azimuth, the height of its day's achievement. The black dial has only dagger hour and minute hands moving around it. Norman Rockwell, the American illustrator, said of the Museum Watch: 'It is so damn' original...a swell, modern, simplified design'.

Five weeks before he died Andy Warhol (owner of 300 watches) completed his picture selection for the five-faced bracelet watch, Times/5. The limited edition was an instant sell-out, and market forces will always keep this amazing conception well into price band [E]. A watch that is steadily moving up from [B] to [C] is the 1940s Calendomatic in 18-carat pink gold. The silvered matt dial of this automatic has applied gold arabic numerals with feuille gold hour and minute hands, a black sweep centre seconds hand and also a date hand pointed towards the outer ring. Month and day windows are above the centre. The bezel is simply moulded and suit the tear-drop lugs.

An unusual 1920s 18-carat gold Polyplan wristwatch by Movado, but with no dial signature. It has a curvex case enclosing a silvered dial with highly stylised arabic numerals. Its slender appearance is accentuated by the position of the crown below 6 o'clock.

OMEGA

The Megaquartz model in Omega's Constellation series. The stainless steel case and bracelet are nicely integrated and set off the starry 'night sky' on the dial.

Omega ('high achievement') dates back to 1848, when Louis Brandt had his assembly shop in La Chaux-de-Fonds. By the 1880s the family firm was prospering in Bienne, producing pocket watches with catchy brand names such as Gurzelen, Helvetia, Jura and Patria. Omega Watch Co was founded in 1903 – the name was suggested by the Brandt's banker – a year after its first wristwatch appeared (with the crown at 9 o'clock).

In both world wars Omega supplied wristwatches to Britain's flying forces. 1948 saw the appearance of its renowned Seamaster, to capitalise on its worldwide reputation for extreme accuracy in timekeeping. Omega's Speedmaster was chosen by NASA for its astronauts in 1965, and Speedmaster Professionals were worn by both American and Russian astronauts during the Apollo-Soyuz space link-up in 1975. Neil Armstrong had worn one on the moon in 1969. Good condition early models of these watches have an obvious attraction. Omega have always produced attractive chronographs. One that is moving up through the price band is the 1930 round 18-carat single-button version with two subsidiary dials at 3 and 9 o'clock. The outer ring is calibrated for pulsation. An associated gold link bracelet keeps the value high, as always. Omega produced, in about 1951, an attractive square 14-carat gold moonphase gentlemen's watch, with a stepped bezel and severe claw-like lugs .

The author's 1938 mechanical Omega resting on the family cat! Cats possess remarkable instincts for accurate timekeeping. This rectangular 18-carat yellow gold curvex model has a raised bevelled sapphire over the gold brushed dial. The subsidiary seconds dial with line markers is at 6 o'clock.

ORIS

A stainless steel case can look attractive if the dial surface is integrated into the overall design - as this Oris mechanical chronograph demonstrates. It has a skeleton back, and is water-resistant to 100 ft (30 m).

Oris was founded in 1904 in the Swiss town of Holstein (where it remains today) by Paul Cattin and Georges Christian. By 1925 they had opened their own electroplating factory, originating what was to become a fine reputation for rolled gold or gold-plating, and from then on produced a succession of middle-of-the-market wristwatches, with some particularly interesting models tucked away among them.

The Oris Wrist Alarms incorporate a limited number of old A.Schild mechanical movements, and are successively numbered. Some of Oris's newer automatics seem very modestly priced: the stainless steel Complication, for example, with moonphase, seconds, day and date dials, and the Automatic Pointer, with its calendar dates beyond the chapter ring [both mid A]. The contemporary Rectangular Classic combines irregular dial markings and has a curved case, and comes in rolled gold or palladium nickel-plated versions [A]. In the early 1960s Oris put out some ladies' wristwatches at very low prices, and typical of the period – fancy but 'safe' cases in varying shapes: round (Bermuda, Hyannis, Jacqueline), tonneau (Adorne) and the usual rectangular. Today such watches should be very inexpensive.

This distinctive Oris automatic, with its tank-style case, dates from 1989. It comes in both palladium-nickel plated brass (above) or gold-plated brass. They have embossed stainless steel backs. The hour markers and index hands are luminous.

PATEK PHILIPPE

Patek Philippe's model 1518 chronograph, produced from 1941 until 1954. This gentlemen's watch has a 30-minute register, perpetual calendar and moonphase indicator.

Mr Patek was Polish and once a typesetter in Cahors; the French-born Philippe trained as a watch maker in Le Havre. Together they set up a watchmaking business in Geneva in 1845. Their names were formally joined on dials in 1851, and Queen Victoria bought one of their watches at the Great Exhibition in London that year. By 1925 Patek Philippe was firmly into the business of producing exquisitely made wristwatches, including the first with perpetual calendars (1925); series production, always in low numbers, only commenced in 1941.

No serious sale room catalogue can fail to feature Patek Philippe wristwatches: and yet just about 50 a day come out of the factory, in various models. Their 'mechanicals', whatever the metal and functions, with their unique numbers, are highly prized all over the world; the 1932 Calatrava for example. Money or love, but not envy, gains them. The [C] band has accessible watches, such as a 1947 18-carat gold rectangular gentleman's model. Uncluttered as ever, the matt silvered dial has raised baton numerals and hands, and a round auxiliary seconds dial at 6 o'clock. Patek Philippe wristwatches are the Rolls-Royces of the wrist, and should only be disposed of in the most dire circumstances. Every so often Patek Philippe reminds the horological trade of its pre-eminence, and in 1985 it patented a Date of Easter display mechanism into its extraordinary Calibre '89 astronomical clock-watch.

Patek Philippe made this platinum minute repeater in about 1929 for Henry Graves, an American sportsman and collector. In 1987 it was sold for 330,000 Swiss francs.

PIAGET

Piaget's mechanical 18-carat gold Dancer comes in a variety of case shapes, but the gold bracelet design remains the same.

Georges Piaget had 14 children and so he had to work hard. In 1874 he set up a small watch movement workshop in the village of La Côte aux Fées above Neuchâtel, gradually enrolling his children as they came of age. But the family did not begin complete watchmaking until after 1945, when Georges' grandsons expanded the business. A very few early 'Piaget & Co' watches are still about, and worth acquiring.

Today Piaget enjoys a distinctive and long-standing reputation for fashion watches. Some are heavily jewelled and not for the temporally pure in taste, or the financially insecure. Indeed, until about 1985 some 70% of annual production was of ladies' watches, and often with dials set with precious stones, whether pavé-style or as hour markers, which became a hallmark of Piaget watches. Often the dial and case design continued over to the bracelet, which is another distinguishing feature of this maker's output. The quartz 1980 Polo sports watch has a modish merger of watch and bracelet showing horizontal gold 'bars' which are alternately matt and polished. The black dial has alternate matt and polished bars as well, just dot seconds markers on the outer ring, gold dauphine hour and minute hands, a gold baton centre sweep seconds hand, and there is a black against white date window at 3 o'clock .

Fashion watches in Piaget's Les Collections Privées are certainly distinctive, and not just for their price tags. The bejewelled bezel around this mother-of-pearl dial has its effect heightened by the simple dauphine hands and the four diamond hour markers.

PULSAR

Pulsar's Pulse/Time Computer which dates from about 1972. They were available from stainless steel versions up to 18-carat yellow gold models.

Early Pulsars seem almost to have been sculpted. The 14-carat gold Pulse/Time Computer model (c.1972), of which only 100 were made, can display your pulse rate on the screen dial simply by you putting your finger tip on the two dots in the black circle at 6 o'clock [B]. You flick your wrist to call up the digital time display on the Auto-Time (1975), and press a button for seconds and the date [A]; the steel version should not be expensive and is fun. The 1972 Time Computer is worth watching out for, in its choice of case metals and bracelets [A].

The 1970 Pulsar Autotime has gained fame, because its brushed rolled gold case is distinctly reminiscent of a television design of the time. The two change buttons are on the broad matching top and bottom lugs and give the date and seconds. The cushion-shaped seemingly black dial displays the time of the day with a shake of the wrist, in red liquid display crystal digits.

This is a classic wristwatch which can often be purchased at the lower end of the [A] price bracket. The 18-carat yellow gold version is more expensive, and the stainless steel one less so.

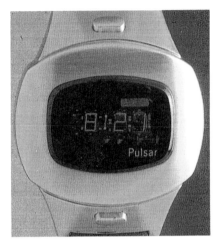

The much admired Autotime (1970) which established Pulsar's name and reputation. Made in various case shapes and bracelets this watch is in 18-carat yellow gold.

RAYMOND WEIL

Raymond Weil's automatic Amadeus 2000 with tachymeter and vigorous push buttons. It was launched in 1984, the year in which the film Amadeus, directed by Milos Forman, was first shown.

This widely promoted maker founded his business with his partner Mrs Simone Bédat as recently as 1976 in Les Brenets, near La Chaux-de-Fonds. His watches are not mechanical marvels or full of innovations, but they are attractive middle-market quartz fashion products which have clearly tapped a demand.

The 1987 Othello range, with eight styles, are ultra-thin and demurely elegant, and would grace any night at the opera, which is just their market. The Traviata line of the following year includes the famous tuning fork across its two-colour numberless dial. Raymond Weil's wristwatches, all in the [A] and [B] bands, are definitely not exclusive products; some 600,000 of them are marketed throughout more than 70 countries each year. In 1984 this maker achieved one of the first quality 'film tie-in' promotions, with its Amadeus model. The Fidelio collection followed the next year. 1990 saw both the launch of the Nabucco and Diva lines and the opening of Raymond Weil's new headquarters in Grand-Lancy, near Geneva. After the Parsifal collection of 1991, Weil produced its first sports watches, and these too bear testimony to original design conceptions.

This round version in Raymond Weil's Parsifal collection is notable for its two screws on the crown protection and also the round (instead of the usual square) date window at 6 o'clock.

REVUE THOMMEN

In 1993 Revue Thommen introduced this skeletonOpen Heart wristwatch. It has an Incabloc movement and the whole case back is transparent, so that all the gear wheels, jewels and bridges are visible. The prominent Louis XV style crown is in robust contrast to the contemporary look of the dial.

This old-established company started life as The Waldenburg Watchmaking Company, in the Swiss town of that name, in 1853. Gédéon Thommen, together with Louis Tschopp, acquired it when he was just 28, in 1858. Soon it was making complete pocket watches, marked GT; in 1910 the Revue label was introduced, and in 1917 the Thommen family commenced wristwatch production.

The first classic watch to come from what is now Revue Thommen was the 1947 Vulcain Cricket. It was the first alarm wristwatch (the on/off button is above the crown) and had been invented by Robert Ditisheim, of Vulcain & Volta, also of La Chaux-de-Fonds (where Revue Thommen was by then based). Ditisheim & Cie, Fabrique Vulcain & Volta had been established there in 1858 by Maurice Ditisheim; it was to become Vulcain & Studio in 1959, and merged with Revue Thommen in 1961. The alarm in the Cricket when it sounds, reproduces the strident sound of a cricket. Nine years after it was re-introduced, in 1986, an edition limited to 850 pieces was issued; it has an 18-carat gold bezel, steel case, Incabloc movement, silvered dial, and a magnified calendar date at 3 o'clock. A line of skeleton watches, in both manual and automatic versions, came on the market in 1966. The 1930s Revue wristwatches were made in large numbers, and the rolled gold tank-like shapes appeal [A].

A modern limited edition replica of Revue Thommen's original 1947 Cricket, the classic alarm wristwatch.

ROLEX

The Rolex Prince, with its two separate dials, is sometimes referred to as a 'doctor's watch'. The Prince is collectable because, since the 1930s, it has appeared with many small variations in case metal combinations and in numeral design.

The famous Rolex name was coined (to sound international) by Bavarian-born Hans Wilsdorf five years after he commenced selling Swiss-made watches from London in 1905. He launched the innovative water-resistant Rolex Oyster in 1927 in Geneva, and successive versions have become collectors' pieces ever since. Today diver's Rolex Oyster Perpetual Submariner (protected to 300m/1000ft) and Sea-Dweller 4000 (1200m/4000ft) models constantly appear in sale rooms.

Other innovations followed. Rolex produced the first watch to incorporate a date (the Datejust) and day together with date (the Day-Date) in windows let into the dials, sometimes with a magnifying bubble of glass over them. Rolex's high output (the firm is Switzerland's biggest industrial user of gold), with a public profile to match, ensures a fast-moving collectors' market – and, alas, ready outlets for this, the most constantly forged brand. A 'wrong' Rolex can look all right on the wrist but it 'feels' quite different from the genuine model. Rolex's luxury line of wristwatches is called Cellini, after the great Renaissance goldsmith. The Geneva company also produces the much less expensive Tudor range of watches. The 1930s Rolex Prince chronometer is one of the most popular models among collectors; a particular favourite is the 18-carat yellow and white gold striped version in a flared rectangular case (it has a slight 'waist' to it) which is 42mm long. It has a two-tone silvered matt face with two dials; the larger upper circle has bold black arabic numerals and black feuille hour and minute hands, while the smaller lower ring has simple baton seconds markers outside it. Prices are now edging towards [E] for mint examples.

The official test certificate supplied in 1930 for a Rolex Prince, from Biel/Bienne, one of Switzerland's great watchmaking centres. All Rolexes are still certified for accuracy today.

ROTARY

A gentlemen's rolled gold quartz watch from Rotary. This Artemis has an exceptionally clean dial, an appearance furthered by the single lugs.

Moise Dreyfuss founded this ever-popular watchmaker (then under his own name) in 1898 in La Chaux-de-Fonds, where it is still located. As the business grew his three sons Georges, René and Sylvain joined him. By 1915 Georges and Sylvain had established a London sales office in the City of London, and René took over from his father in 1925. He continued to work until he was 93. In the following year they together established the brand name Rotary (which was to become the company's name in 1956).

It was in the early 1920s that the brothers realised the potential of rolled gold for watch cases, and set about making classic-looking watches of all kinds which they were able to retail at very competitive prices in many parts of the world. Rotary were among the first makers to sell through department stores in Switzerland. At one time Rotary was merged with Longines, and also owned Roamer (founded 1888); neither arrangement lasted. In memory of the founder's son the René Dreyfuss collection of mechanical wristwatches appeared in 1982, and it included an hour and five minute chiming repeater. Another celebratory range is the 1898, which have round quartz movements and date windows. Gemini is the name of Rotary's quartz complicated watches. Among their more recent output is the Vogue watch which has a particularly wide polished bezel in either rolled gold or nickel palladium; their dials are either with dot numerals or without any, and the hands are chubby little dauphines.

Rotary's Khalif quartz multi-function chronograph in rolled gold.

SEIKO

The large milled and protected crown on this 1987 Seiko (the year of its launch) proclaims that it is a hand-winding model. It has a quartz movement and its charge indicator is at 6 o'clock.

This Japanese brand name is a shortened form of Seikosha Co. Ltd. which was founded in 1892. It was later to be acquired by H. Hattori & Co. Ltd (which had been formed in 1881) and it still makes clocks and other timing systems. Today wristwatches are made by Seiko Instruments and Electronics Ltd (1937) and Suwa Seikosha Co. Ltd (1942); subsidiary brands include Pulsar, Jean Lassale and Yema Paris.

Seiko's place in horological history is secure because it produced the world's first commercial quartz wristwatch in 1969. The Astron incorporated – for the technically minded – 76 transistors, 29 capacitors, an oscillator and 83 printed resistors in a movement which was 11mm thick, with 128 soldered connections. That watch led the 'quartz revolution' which gave the Swiss watch trade such a fright in the early and mid-1970s. Seiko's wristwatch production (for men) commenced in 1913; ladies' watches followed in 1927. Other 'firsts' for the company include their quartz 18-carat gold watch (1972), an LCD digital quartz watch (1973), the world's first TV watch (1982), its own first voice memo watch (1983), the first computer component watch (1984), its first hand-wound quartz model (1987), and, in 1988, the Seiko AGS (Automatic Generating System). This is powered by the world's first automatic generator which is activated solely by the watch wearer's arm movements.

A straightforward quartz Seiko wristwatch for fans of digital timepieces. The change buttons are below the LCD window.

SWATCH

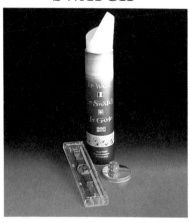

On 12 February 1994, 118 people walked through the Channel Tunnel from Calais to Folkestone and raised nearly £2m for charities. Swatch was the official timekeeper and commemorated the event by producing 3100 Swatch chronographs - 100 for every mile of the way. The Andale and Metal Flash models were in a presentation tube with a fantasy game. Le Walk will never occur again, and these watches will be highly collectable.

Swatches were the brainchild of Nicolas G. Hayek who had been trying to uncover a Swiss response for his company, SMH, to the Japanese invasion of his traditional markets with their quartz movement watches in the five years since 1978. They have since become a pop-cultural phenomenon, and in 1992 some 27 million were sold, making a total of over 150 million to March 1994.

About 140 different Swatches are designed each year, and certainly the different market places are having a confusing time pin-pointing the classic sellers, which incorporate the special 51 part movements of Elmar Mock and Jacques Muller. The all-time star is the Kiki Picasso (1985) [E]. The original 1984 Jellyfish, the Royal Puff [D], the set of three Vegetables, called Swatchetables (999 only, vacuum-packed, with sell-by dates!), and the 1985 Sir Limelight [B] are enviable Swatch models. Rising stars include the 1991 Hocus Pocus, Gulp and Crash [all A]. A spectacular star in the ascendant is the 1989 design by Mimmo Paladino, limited to 120 watches [E]. Late in 1993 the Trésor Magique was launched in a worldwide limited edition of 12,999; this platinum automatic chronometer came with interchangeable mock-croc straps, and retailed at £1000, or currency equivalent, each. The 'Swatch Collectors of Swatch' Club in the UK is at SMH UK Ltd, Empress Road, Bevois Valley, Southampton, Hants SO9 7DS. Children's Flik-Flak watches also come out of the SMH stable.

Three Heavy Metal Swatches which were produced in late 1988.

TAG-HEUER

TAG-Heuer's S/el (Sports Elegance) range was launched in 1988. In 1993 came this S/el Leather, which has certain differences in the case and dial (which here has a sixth colour). It comes with either quartz or automatic movement, in a choice of six strap colours.

TAG stands for Techniques d'Avant-Garde, which is a Paris-based technology investment company founded in 1977. It is particularly involved with Formula One Grand Prix motor racing. The watch-making company that Edouard Heuer founded in St Imier in 1860 has long been involved in sports event timekeeping; it was for example the official appointee of the Antwerp Olympic Games in 1920. TAG-Heuer was formed in 1985; the next year saw a Formula One sports watch in fibreglass and steel, which happily coincided with Alain Prost's world drivers' championship in his Marlboro McLaren TAG Turbo.

In 1987 TAG-Heuer launched, from Bienne, a new range of sports watches called S/el (Sports Elegance), and the S/el Leather line came in 1993. These quartz watches are in steel or gold plate and either with or without a uni-directional turning bezel with ratchet. Sports watch collectors are aware of the wide range that Heuer manufactured in the 1930s and 1940s [A to

B] – from simple chronographs with one subsidiary dial to, for example, the multi-dialled 1932 steel chronograph with tachymetre [B]. Later, in 1970, Heuer produced the Autavia, which was an automatic chronograph for divers, motorists and pilots. The outer bezel on the Autavia MH rotated giving comparisons between time zones, departure and arrival times, and elapsed and remaining oxygen consumption.

The B model in TAG-Heuer's 6000 series, in brushed stainless steel and 18-carat gold. It has a unidirectional turning bezel, screwed-in crown, luminous dial indicators, and is water-resistant down to 600ft (200m)

TIFFANY

This Atlas watch from Tiffany is rugged like the mountain range, and the dial is of the minimalist variety. This 18-carat yellow gold model has a sterling silver counterpart.

Charles Lewis Tiffany started selling watches and clocks in his soon-to-be famous New York stationery and fancy goods store in 1847, ten years after he had opened. Soon he was being supplied from Switzerland by Mr Patek and Mr Philippe (who formally joined together in 1851). In 1872 Charles Tiffany opened a watchmaking factory in Geneva, and it soon became the largest in Switzerland. Those were the days of the famous Tiffany Timer, an accurate chronograph for travel and sports timing.

Prices for Tiffany's jewelled ladies' wristwatches of the Art Deco period can vary enormously according to the stones and their quality. Very small square-cased and tonneau curvexes, perhaps with a modest setting around the bezel, can still be found in the [A] range. In the 1940s Tiffany was producing a moonphase calendar chronograph, with a gold-coloured main dial, a subsidiary seconds dial, and day and month windows below 12 o'clock [B]. The mid-

1950s brought a range of ultra-thin dress watches in 18-carat gold with elegant black suede straps. These mostly had baton numerals and hands, but with the occasional 12 o'clock depicted [B]. In 1965 the Classics collection was launched, with each watch bearing, as ever, 'Tiffany & Co' on the dial. The company's 150th anniversary in 1987 was celebrated with its Tesoro collection, in 18-carat gold, or gold with stainless steel, and three years later Tiffany established (for the second time) its own watch factory in Switzerland.

Tiffany stands for boxed gifts of quality. This Tesoro chronograph has a quartz movement and also comes in 18-carat gold and in stainless steel. The date window has an unusual position.

TISSOT

Three of the Tissot Rock Watches produced in 1992 in a limited and numbered edition of 1300 pieces.

In 1853 Charles-Emile Tissot returned to Le Locle after a five year stay in New York and persuaded his father Charles-Félicien to open a watch factory with him. The early American makers were, the younger Tissot noted, great exporters, and the first-ever Tissot watches were duly sold in the United States. Soon Russia became Tissot's biggest market – but that was promptly closed in 1917.

Tissot was ahead of the industry with its 1930 antimagnetic wristwatch. In 1944 Paul Tissot's automatic (self-winding) watch came, at a time when, by now based in Bienne, he was perfecting its production lines (he was the co-founder's grandson). The Tissot Navigator, which was the first automatic with an international calendar, was followed by the extra water-resistant Tissot 12. The 1958 watch collection, for the first time, was confined to a single calibre, which enabled Tissot to keep its watch prices in the [A] range. This policy continues, and at that end of the market Tissot has been most innovatory. In 1970 Tissot achieved a plastic movement with only 52 parts (instead of over 90 for metal movements). The RockWatch, launched in 1985, has enduring appeal, and its arboreal equivalent, the WoodWatch, followed in 1988. It is made of Corsican briar, which is also used for top-quality pipes. No two of these watches can ever be the same. In between these, in 1987, Tissot's TwoTimer chronograph came out, featuring day and date, the time in another chosen time zone, a timer with countdown, and a 24-hour alarm.

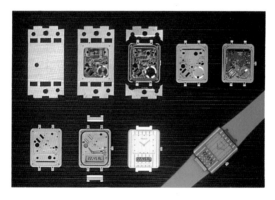

Components of Tissot's revolutionary TwoTimer (1987), with its two time displays, one analogue and one digital.

ULYSSE NARDIN

The Planetarium Copernicus is a typically complicated watch from Ulysse Nardin. It indicates the minute, hour, day, month, moon phases and astronomical positions of the sun, moon and largest planets, current zodiac sign, and the respective astrological positions of the planets in terms of degrees (as observed from the earth) showing relevant 'aspects'.

This award-winning company was formed by Ulysse Nardin in 1846 in his native Le Locle to make pocket chronometers and alarm watches for naval officers. That market disappeared after 1945. Since 1983 Rolf W. Schnyder has revived the company by producing splendidly complicated wristwatches, to succeed earlier and less expensive ones. The Astrolabium Galileo Galilei (1988) is so accurate that, after 144,000 years, it will show only one day's deviation from the stars' precise positions [E].

Ulysse Nardin makes about 4,000 timepieces a year in over 40 models. If, therefore, you can afford their high prices you are certainly acquiring limited editions of engineering marvels. The dial of the Planetarium Copernicus (1988) combines the heliocentric universe of Nicolaus Copernicus with Ptolemy's geocentric universe. Its matt grey dial indicates the astronomical position of the sun and moon, and has concentric circles each representing a planet. The outer gilt ring gives the months and zodiac signs, and the bezel of this round automatic 18-carat gold wristwatch has incised roman numerals [E]. Seriously wealthy collectors and investors should address themselves to the 18-carat gold Split Second Chronograph. Each is individually numbered on the dial; ten were made in white gold, 20 in yellow gold, and 30 in pink gold. There are though hundreds of much more prosaic but attractive Ulysse Nardin watches from the 1920-1965 period.

This minute repeater from Ulysse Nardin incorporates a reproduction of the animated clockwork of Venice's San Marco clock tower. The 18-carat gold dial is covered with blue enamel. The bell at 12 o'clock is struck by the two golden male figures with hammers at the hours and quarters.

UNIVERSAL GENÈVE

The standard Uni-Compax model in Universal Genève's Compax range of chronographs. This modern piece is based on the original 1950s design and specifications.

George Perret, a Le Locle-based watchmaker, started his business in 1894. Louis Berthoud became his partner in 1897, and, as Perret & Berthoud, first distributed and then manufactured pocket watches and later wristwatches. Soon they moved to Geneva. In 1917 they marketed the first bracelet chronograph. Guided by Raoul Perret, George's grandson, the business was refinanced in 1934 and adopted the name Universal Genève. In the same year it launched the first chronograph with two push pieces and a 17 ligne movement.

Collectors should look out for early (beginning of the 1950s) Compax models in good condition. The 18-carat yellow gold Tri-Compax chronograph of about 1955 is water-resistant, and its silvered dial, with gold raised baton numerals (none at the quarters), gold dauphine hour and minute hands and a black sweep seconds hand, features four subsidiary dials at the quarters [D]. The dials indicate constant seconds, registers for 30 minutes and 12 hours and date, combined with moon phases, and it also has day and month windows. Other models in this classic range include the Compax, Medico Compax (in which the outer ring is calibrated for pulsations) and Uni-Compax (which has a tachymetre). The Aerocompax was a pilot's watch (with an extra dial for recording a departure time), and, like all the others, had an Incabloc anti-shock device. The company's Tuning Ultrasonic, launched in 1968, was the first electronic wristwatch with a tuning fork.

An 18-carat rose gold Tri-Compax Universal Genève full calendar moonphase chronograph; the baton and arabic hour markers alternate - interrupted periodically at 12 o'clock by a gloomy lunar face.

VACHERON CONSTANTIN

A world-timer from Vacheron Constantin. This is the 18-carat gold automatic Phidias with an integrated gold bracelet.

Jean-Marc Vacheron was only 24 when he opened a watch workshop in 1755 in Geneva. His grandson, Jacques-Barthélemy Vacheron, took on François Constantin as a partner in 1819; the latter loved travelling and selling, which is how their pocket watches were selling in America by 1833 and India by 1847. The Maltese cross symbol arrived on their dials in 1880. The first Vacheron Constantin wristwatch came in 1910, and exquisite models have been coming from their factory ever since. But this is another maker the annual output of which is well under 10,000 units – and each one is individually numbered.

Vacheron Constantin (sometimes '&' appears between the names on dials) has always produced expensive watches, but, as with other prestigious brands, they appear with regularity and in quantity in the sale rooms. The middle of the [B] price band would bring a secondhand (or, previously owned, to quote the now correct expression) 1954 round 18-carat automatic chronometer with the maker's typical design: a white enamel dial, with applied gold baton numerals and gold baton hour, minute and sweep seconds hands. Once windows and subsidiary dials appear the prices spiral upwards. Collectors of early ladies' jewelled watches will know that this maker produced some elegant rectangular platinum-cased wristwatches, set with diamonds and sapphires, which basically dictate the price, and generally they were not signed on the front dial.

This 1970s Vacheron Constantin ladies' chronometer typifies the understated style of this Geneva maker. The elaborate arabic numerals are exactly complemented by the losange hands.

ZENITH

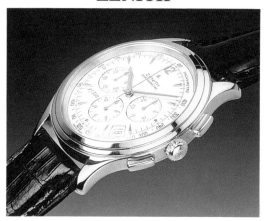

*Zenith's El Primero, launched in 1969, with its unique move-
ment (see opposite), which has 280 components.*

This Le Locle-based maker has been winning watch
awards ever since Georges Favre-Jacot formed the
business in 1865 – in fact, over 1500 of them! Zenith
was one of the earliest Swiss companies both to
advertise and market vigorously in Great Britain a
wide range of middle-market wristwatches.

The one watch with which Zenith will always be
associated is the El Primero (1969). It housed the
world's first automatic chronograph movement; the
fast beat spring balance vibrates 36,000 times an hour,
which is ten times per second. Today's automatic
version (available in a variety of metals, bracelets, dial
colours, etc.) has a continuously moving sweep seconds hand, a date window between 4 and 5 o'clock,
and the three subsidiary dials give short time measurements to 1/10ths of a second, 30 minutes and hours. A
tachymetre is featured on the bezel on some models
and outside the chapter ring on others. The Calibre
410 version has a moon phase indicator and is made
up of 354 components, of which 277 are different.

The world's first automatic chronograph movement and the only one of its kind to carry out short time measurement to a tenth of a second - the calibre 400 for Zenith's El Primero. Zenith manufacture all their own mechanical movements, and also assemble their quartz ones.

Useful Addresses

BRITAIN

**ANTIQUARIAN
HOROLOGICAL SOCIETY**
New House
High Street
Ticehurst
East Sussex TN5 7AL
Tel:(0580) 200155

BONHAMS
Auctioneers
Montpelier Galleries
Montpelier Street
London SW7 1HH
Tel:(071) 584 9161
Fax:(071) 589 4072

BONHAMS CHELSEA
Auctioneers
65-69 Lots Road
London SW10 0RN
Tel:(071) 351 7111
Fax:(071) 351 7754

**BRITISH HOROLOGICAL
INSTITUTE**
Upton Hall
Upton
Newark
Nottinghamshire NG23 5TE
Tel:(0636) 813795/6
Fax:(0636) 812258

CHRISTIE'S
Auctioneers
8 King Street
St James's
London SW1Y 6QT
Tel:(071) 839 9060
Fax:(071) 839 1611

CHRISTIE'S
Auctioneers
85 Old Brompton Road
South Kensington
London SW7 3LD
Tel:(071) 581 7611
Fax:(071) 321 3321

'CLOCKS'
Argus Specialist Publications
Argus House
Boundary Way
Hemel Hempstead
Herts HP2 7ST
Tel:0442 66551
Fax:0442 66998

HOROLOGICAL FAIRS
—Enquire for venues and dates
PO Box 273
Uxbridge
Middlesex UB9 4LP
Tel:(0895) 834357
Fax:(0895) 832329

**'INTERNATIONAL
WRISTWATCH'**
Hallmark Publications Ltd
Hyde Park House
5 Manfred Road
London SW15 2RS
Tel:(081) 877 1080
Fax:(081) 874 2150

PHILLIPS, SON & NEALE
Auctioneers
101 New Bond Street
London W1Y 0AS
Tel:(071) 629 6602
Fax:(071) 629 8876

**PRESCOT MUSEUM OF
WATCH AND
CLOCKMAKING**
34 Church Street
Prescot
Knowsley
Lancashire L34 3LA
Tel:(051) 430 7787
Fax:(051) 430 7219

'RETAIL JEWELLER'
67 Clerkenwell Road
London EC1R 5BH
Tel:(071) 404 2763
Fax:(071) 404 2764

SOTHEBY'S
Auctioneers
34-35 New Bond Street
London W1A 2AA
Tel:(071) 493 8080
Fax:(071) 409 3100
Telex:24454 SPBLON G

SOTHEBY'S
Auctioneers
Summers Place
Billingshurst
Sussex RH14 9AD
Tel:(0403) 783933
Fax:(0403) 785153

THE WORSHIPFUL COMPANY OF CLOCKMAKERS
Clock and Watch Collection
Guildhall Library
Aldermanbury
London EC2P 2EJ
Open: Mon-Fri 9.30-4.45

FRANCE

'INTERNATIONAL HEURE MAGAZINE'
Veda-Editions Challenge
42 Avenue Kléber
75116 Paris
Tel:(1) 47550084
Fax:(1) 47556641

MILLON & ROBERT
19 rue de la Grange Batelière
75009 Paris
Tel:(1) 48 00 99 44
Fax:(1) 48 00 98 58

GERMANY

BITTIG PROMOTIONS
Auctioneers/Swap Shops
Internationale Frankfurter
Uhrenbörse
Galgenfeld 53
W-6384 Schmitten
Tel:(0) 6084 2197

'INTERNATIONAL WRISTWATCH'
Heel-Verlag GMbH
Haupstrasse 354
5330 Königswinter 1
Tel:(0) 2223/23027
Fax:(0) 2223/23028

'UHREN'
Streitfeld Strasse 35
D-81673 Munich
Tel:(89) 4360050
Fax:(89) 43600513

HOLLAND

CHRISTIE'S
Cornelis Schuystraat 57
1071 JG, Amsterdam
- Correspondence to:
PO Box 53005
1007 RA, Amsterdam
Tel:(3120) 575 5255
Fax;(3120) 664 0899

SOTHEBY'S
Auctioneers
102 Rokin
1012 KZ Amsterdam
Tel:(020) 6275656
Fax:(020) 6201057

ITALY

CHRISTIE'S
Palazzo Massimo Lancellotti
Piazza Navona 114
00186 Rome
Tel:(396) 687 2787
Fax;(396) 689 3080

'OROLOGI DA POLSO'
Edizioni Studio Zeta Srl
via S Fruttuoso 10
20052 Monza (MI)
Tel:(039) 736451
Fax:(039) 736500

JAPAN

'INTERNATIONAL WRIST-WATCH'
Nigensha Publishing Co Ltd
2-2 Kanda-Jimbocho
Chiyoda-ku
Tokyo 101
Tel:(813) 5275-0191
Fax:(813) 5275-0192

MONACO

ORION AUCTION HOUSE
13 Bd. Princesse Charlotte
Monte Carlo
MC 98000 Monaco
Tel:(93) 301669
Fax:(93) 501792

SWITZERLAND

ANTIQUORUM
Auctioneers
1 rue du Mont-Blanc
CH-1201 Genève
Tel:(022) 738 02 22
Fax:(022) 738 01 71

CHRISTIE'S
Auctioneers
8 place de la Taconnerie
CH-1204 Genève
Tel:(022) 311 1766
Fax;(022) 311 5559/5006

MUSÉE D'HORLOGERIE
Château des Monts
CH-2400 Le Locle
Tel:(039) 31 16 80
Fax:(039) 31 42 31

**MUSÉE D'HORLOGERIE
ET DE L'EMAILLERIE**
Route de Malagnon 15
1208 Genève
Tel:(022) 36 74 12
Fax:(022) 786 74 54

**MUSÉE INTERNATIONAL
D'HORLOGERIE**
Rue des Musées 29
La Chaux-de-Fonds
Tel:(039) 23 62 63
Fax:(039) 23 49 90

SOTHEBY'S
Auctioneers
13 Quai du Mont-Blanc
CH-1201 Genève
Tel:(022) 732 85 85
Fax:(022) 731 65 94

TAIWAN

CHRISTIE'S
6F-5 Floor, 369 Fu-Hsing
North Road
Taipei 10483
Taipei R.O.C.
Tel:(8862) 718 1612
Fax:(0862) 718 3702

U.S.A.

**BUTTERFIELD &
BUTTERFIELD**
Auctioneers
7601 Sunset Boulevard
Los Angeles
CA 90046
Tel:(213) 850 7500
Fax:(213) 850 5843

**BUTTERFIELD &
BUTTERFIELD**
Auctioneers
220 San Bruno Avenue
San Francisco
CA 94103
Tel:(415) 861 7500
Fax:(415) 861 8951

CHRISTIE'S
Auctioneers
502 Park Avenue
New York NY 10022
Tel:(212) 546 1000
Fax:(212) 980 8163/8173

CHRISTIE'S EAST
219 East 67th Street
New York
NY 10021
Tel:(212) 606 0400
Fax:(212) 737 6076

**'INTERNATIONAL
WRISTWATCH'**
International Publishers Corp
242 West Avenue
Darien, CT 06820
Tel:(203) 656 3913
Fax:(203) 656 2774

`MODERN JEWELER'
Vance Publishing
7950 College Boulevard
Overland Park
Kansas 66210
Tel: (913) 451 2200
Fax: (913) 451 5821

**NATIONAL ASSOCIATION
OF WATCH AND CLOCK
COLLECTORS INC**
514 Poplar Street
Columbia
Pennsylvania 17512-2130
Tel:(717) 684 8261
Fax:(717) 684 0878

SOTHEBY'S
Auctioneers
1334 York Avenue
New York NY 10021
Tel:(212) 606 7000
Fax:(212) 606 7107

THE TIME MUSEUM
7801 East State Street
PO Box 5285
Rockford
Illinois 61125-0285
Tel:(815) 398 6000
Fax:(815) 398 4700

INDEX

Makers in **bold** type are specially featured. Page numbers in *italics* indicate illustrations.